NEW MEXICO

Historic Marker Roadmaps

EL RITO

Elevation 6,870 ft.

This village was settled in the
1830s by residents from the
Abiquiú area. The Territorial
Legislature of 1909 established
the Spanish-American Normal
School here to train teachers for
northern New Mexico schools.
After several changes in name
and purpose, the institution is
now the Northern New Mexico
Community College.

*Inspiring Stories of Men,
Women and Places*

Phil T. Archuletta and
Rosanne Roberts Archuletta

Published in the United States by the authors, Phil T. Archuletta and Rosanne Roberts Archuletta
www.travelingnewmexico.com
www.pmsignsinc.com
www.womenmarkedforhistory.com

ISBN (paperback): 979-8-9873053-0-0
eISBN: 979-8-9873053-1-7
Library of Congress Control Number: 2022922157

Cover Design: Krista Dunk, www.100xPublishing.com
Book Cover Photo: Historic Marker – El Rito, New Mexico
Installation site: NM 554 in El Rito on the Northern New Mexico College El Rito campus

Dedication

This book is dedicated to the Northern New Mexico College's El Rito Campus. It has played an important role in New Mexico's goal of providing educational opportunities in rural communities.

Initially the school in El Rito was known as the Spanish American Normal School. It was both a day school and a boarding school, providing secondary and post-secondary educational programs to its students. In 1959 the school was renamed the Northern New Mexico College continuing to teach grades 7 through 12, in addition to adding a new college curriculum.

In 1969 the high school curriculum was transferred to a newly created public school district and the curriculum at the College became limited to technical-vocational course offerings. At that time the school was renamed the New Mexico Technical-Vocational School, indicating the change in the courses being offered.

As of 2023, the name of the school has returned to the Northern New Mexico College. The main campus is located in Española with the buildings on the El Rito campus available for community events. There are ongoing discussions about the possibility of offering classes on the El Rito campus once again.

Table of Contents

Foreword

There can be an argument made that yesterday is more important than either today or tomorrow. Events, experiences, and people from the past, no matter how insignificant some may say they are, mold the path of the future. The lessons learned from the past construct what happens today and tomorrow.

Throughout the State of New Mexico, historical markers are scattered along the scenic routes where historically significant events have occurred. These markers briefly describe the events, experiences and people that have made this State what it is today. Some markers describe heroic actions that we hope are repeated, some describe tragic events that we hope will never happen again and others describe how the communities that make up this great State came into existence. These markers provide an introduction into the significance, both culturally and historically, of the past and gives tourists, visitors, and residents alike an opportunity to learn about the cultural and history of our great State.

The New Mexico Historical Marker Project's importance cannot be overstated. Past, current, and future generations benefit from the information contained within markers. As one drives through the plains, deserts or mountainous regions within New Mexico, the beauty of the scenery speaks for itself. However, the historical markers speak for the past. The historical contributions by these groups, communities, men and women are just as important as the beauty of our state's terrain. I strongly encourage everyone to take the time to stop, look around, read these markers, and learn from our past to mold a better tomorrow.

Andrew J. Gallegos P.E.
Traffic Operations Engineer
New Mexico Department of Transportation
Santa Fe, New Mexico

Phil and Rosanne Archuletta's Acknowledgements

New Mexico Department of Transportation
  Ricky Serna, Secretary
  Rick Padilla, Executive Director of Highway Operations
  Jerry P. Valdez, Executive Director
  John Romero, Highway Operations Support Division Director
  Joseph De La Rosa, Director of Public Service
  Andrew Gallegos, Traffic Operations Engineer
  Mershawn Griego, Administrator

New Mexico Cultural Affairs office – Historic Preservation Division
  Debra Garcia y Griego, Cabinet Secretary for Department of Cultural Affairs
  Jeff Pappas, PhD, State Historic Preservation Officer

Personal and Professional Acknowledgements
  Maybel and Lizandro Ocaña and their son, Lee, for their belief in Phil and all of his projects.
  Larry Archuleta for supporting Phil throughout his lifetime. His wife and Phil's sister Bertha Archuleta, for her edits of the original manuscript of this book
  Leroy Pacheco, President and CEO of The Loan Fund, for generously sharing all of Phil and Rosanne's books with his clients.
  Krista Dunk, Author Coach, Book Publisher and Editor
  Nancy Smith, Amy Beattie, Chris Urso, Gracia Coffin, Deon Douglas, Patty Palmer Rutt, Gwendolyn Rogers, Debby Stein, Norman Roberts, Rick Roberts, Patricia Roberts, Doreen Lipare, LeeAnn Trexler, Pat Pearson, Melissa Loson, Mary Tanner, Debbie Collins, Sharon Miller, Kelly Corah, Katie Corah, Patricia Forbes, Tom Miles, Denise Chavez, Father Elias, Janine Jones, Marie Bush, Patti Bray, Anne Hilyard Goetz, Carine Camara, Chris Roberts, Ben DiFilippi, Kevin Mummau, Mark Hoaglin, and Rev. Brendalyn Batchelor for the support they have offered Rosanne during the writing of this book, her two other books, and developing and managing her consulting business over the years.

Introduction

This new Historic Marker book, *New Mexico Historic Marker Roadmaps: Inspiring Stories of Men, Women and Places,* is a compilation of new and revised road side markers from the last decade. In this book, you'll find maps with the location of each marker, the text of the marker and other significant information. The texts of the Markers are reviewed by the Historic Preservation office about every ten years. Sometimes there are no changes to the text and at other times the text is rewritten for clarity or to add or remove a statement.

Our intention is that you'll find our New Mexico history fascinating, leaving you with the desire to learn more. We have provided a list of additional resources at the end of the book to assist you in your exploration of our enchanting state.

We have two other New Mexico Historic Marker books. *Traveling New Mexico* was written by Phil Archuletta and was published in 2004. Phil and Rosanne Archuletta published *Women Marked for History* in 2013. This book won the New Mexico Historic Preservation Award in 2015.

Our goal is that you'll plan trips to visit the sites of the places where these incredible people lived, and historic battles and events took place.

We also hope that you'll be inspired by our stories to become more active in your own life and community, or perhaps act on a dream that you have long forgotten.

History of the New Mexico Historical Marker Project
(1935 – Present)

1935: The Historical Marker Project was created in 1935. Initially, the Markers were manufactured by the State Highway Department and the New Mexico Prison Industries. The vigas were constructed according to the drawings of the State Highway Department, and Sotenes Delgado, an employee of the department printed the panels.

1972: Phil Archuletta, the co-author of this book, while a senior executive at Ojo Caliente Craftsmen, was given a contract by the State Highway Department to cut the Juniper vigas that were used in the manufacturing of the Historical Marker structure.

1980: The Federal Highway Department required a change to New Mexico Historical Markers. The original signs, which were in the colors of yellow, black, red and green, were not compliant with a new federal law requiring these type of signs to be colored in brown and white.

1981: The Cultural Review Committee and the New Mexico State Highway Department awarded another contract to Phil Archuletta's company, Ojo Caliente Craftsmen. His company was to redesign and manufacture the Historical Markers following the specifications of the new federal law.

1994: P & M Signs, Inc., in Mountainair, New Mexico, owned by Phil Archuletta and his business partners, Maybel and Lizandro Ocaña, was awarded a new contract to continue the manufacturing of the New Mexico Historical Markers.

2005: There was approval by the New Mexico Legislature to fund 64 markers containing women's contributions to the history of the state for the first time.

· Bernalillo County ·

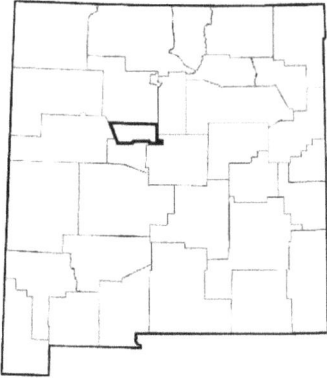

Created in 1852 as one of the nine original counties, this county was named after the settlement of Bernalillo.

County Seat: Albuquerque

Communities: Chilili, Tijeras, Cedar Crest, Alameda and Rio Rancho

1,169 Square Miles

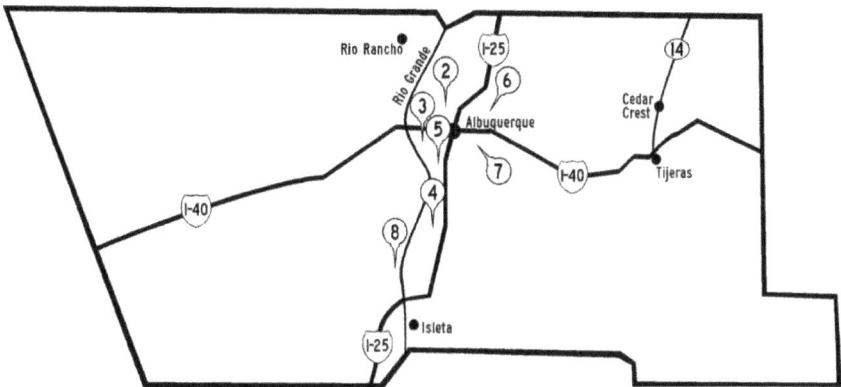

ALAMEDA

A Tiwa pueblo was located in this area prior to Francisco Vàzquez de Coronado's arrival in 1540 and Juan de Oñate's colonizing expedition in 1598. A 1680 Spanish inventory recorded 300 Tiwas at the pueblo. The Spanish named the area Alameda. The name derives from the Spanish word for cottonwood, likely referring to the groves lining the Camino Real. Following the Pueblo Revolt of 1680, the pueblo was abandoned, and the following year was burned.

Tiwas briefly inhabited the pueblo in 1702 and abandoned it in 1709 when the residents moved to Isleta Pueblo. In 1710 Francisco Montes Vigil petitioned for the Town of Alameda Grant, which was approved by Governor José Chacón Salazar y Villaseñor. Alameda remained a Hispanic farming community from the 18th through the 21st centuries and today is an unincorporated community in Albuquerque's north valley.

This Spanish settlement was established initially on the site of an ancient Tiwa Indian Pueblo that was destroyed following the Pueblo Revolt of 1680. The pueblo was then reestablished in 1702, but in 1709 the Spanish moved its Tiwa inhabitants to help resettle the Pueblo of Isleta.

Alameda's original Catholic church began as a Mission known as Nativity of Our Lady (or Alameda Chapel of the Immaculate Conception). It was located east of the Alameda Bridge and north of Rio Grande

Boulevard and Alameda Boulevard. A flood in 1903 destroyed the church.

In 1912, the present-day Nativity of the Blessed Virgin Mary located at 4th Street and Alameda Boulevard was completed.

Installation Site

Intersection of 4th and 2nd Streets in the Alameda Community of Albuquerque

ALBUQUERQUE

In 1706 New Mexico Governor Francisco Cuervo y Valdés founded the Villa de Alburquerque (now spelled Albuquerque), which became the principal settlement of the Rio Abajo, or lower river district. Here, the Camino Real wound its way through a series of farming and ranching communities and led to a nearby ford, which linked the Camino Real to settlements on the west bank of the Rio Grande.

Albuquerque was the main commercial center for the Rio Grande valley until the 1880 arrival of the railroad, one-and-a-half miles east of the plaza. Growth and development centered on the railroad and "New" Albuquerque. Now known as Plaza Vieja or Old Town, the plaza, plan of narrow streets, and historic buildings are representative of a traditional Hispanic city.

Albuquerque, located in the high desert, is New Mexico's largest city. Over the years, it has become a modern city, yet has kept its roots. Old Town Albuquerque, located just west of downtown, consists of historic adobe buildings housing restaurants and shops. Nearby the Pueblo Culture Center is a reminder of the area's tribal roots.

Installation Site

On the plaza in Old Town Albuquerque facing North Plaza Street NW

CAMP ALBUQUERQUE

Camp Albuquerque was established for German prisoners transferred from New Mexico's main POW camp in Roswell. The prisoners were initially housed in a former Civilian Conservation Corps barracks in Albuquerque. City leader Clyde Tingley reinforced prevailing public sentiment, vehemently opposing German soldiers living in city limits. He struck a deal with feedlot owner Joe Schwartzman who donated land near here to relocate the barracks. The prisoners, captured in North Africa as part of the renowned Afrika Korps, became valued workers assisting Rio Grande Valley farmers feed the state and nation.

Camp Albuquerque was an American World War II Prison of War camp located in Albuquerque, housing Italian and German prisoners of war. At the peak, sometime in 1945, there were nearly 200 German POWs in the camp. The prisoners worked harvesting the produce on local area farms.

Installation Site
At Bernalillo County South Valley Rail Runner Station

DOÑA ELENA GALLEGOS ELENA GALLEGOS LAND GRANT (1680 – 1731)

Doña Elena Gallegos was the daughter of early seventeenth-century Hispanic colonists, Antonio Gallegos and Catalina Baca. They fled New Mexico with their newborn daughter during the 1680 Pueblo Revolt but returned in 1692. Elena wed Santiago Gurulé, a tattooed Frenchman, born Jacques Grolet, a member of the ill-fated La Salle expedition. Everyone with the Hispanized form of his surname, Gurulé, has roots in New Mexico. Approximately two years after her husband's death in 1712, Captain Diego Montoya conveyed to Elena the vast landholding that has since born her name.

From the crest of the Sandia Mountains to the Rio Grande Valley lies the Elena Gallegos Land Grant. It covered 70,000 acres, approximately the northern half of Albuquerque up to Sandia Pueblo. The extent of the grant – some felt its eastern border was the foothills – was uncertain until a nineteenth-century court interpreted the word "sierra" in the original document as the crest of the mountains. The adjudication helped make it possible to preserve part of the land grant as open space and provide a picnic area for the enjoyment of all.

The Elena Gallegos Land Grant covered 70,000 acres. This land grant consisted of the northern half of Albuquerque to Sandia Pueblo. The exact area covering the land grant was disputed until a nineteenth-century court made a final decision. Their verdict helped make it possible to preserve part of the land grant as open space, keeping it available to the citizens of Albuquerque. Today, this open space which consists of a park and trail areas, is still enjoyed by locals and tourists alike.

Installation Site
Elena Gallegos Open Space and Picnic Grounds – 7100 Tramway Blvd NE, Albuquerque

FLAMENCO
"THE DANCE OF PASSION"
Clarita Garcia de Aranda Allison
(1921 – 1989)

Flamenco is a dance of fiery passion and great skill, believed to have originated in Andalucia, Spain, in the fifteenth century and to have taken root in New Mexico in part due to the state's historic and cultural ties to Spain. The flamenco tradition was taught and performed in the early twentieth century in family and community gatherings and still enjoyed throughout the state in public celebrations of Hispanic heritage. The University of New Mexico is the first and only institute of higher education in the world to offer degrees in flamenco.

Among the most renown teachers and performers of flamenco in the state, Carital grew up in a musical family and was heavily influenced by her mother and her brother Antonio, a professional dancer. After serving as a civilian Spanish-language interpreter in World War II, Clarita opened a dance school in Albuquerque. Clarita's School of Dance, leading her students in performance around the state as the Baile Flamenco. Her love for the flamenco tradition brought greater awareness and appreciation to this centuries-old art form and its importance in the cultural history of the Southwest.

Flamenco is a professional dance art form created by Spanish gypsies, known as Gitanos, in the late 1800s. Flamenco is based on various folk music traditions of southern Spain in Andalusia, Extremadura, and Murcia communities. It continues to grow throughout New Mexico and the world by practitioners who continue to sustain this beautiful art form with authenticity and integrity.

Installation Site
University of New Mexico campus –
near Popejoy Hall

JOSEFA BACA
PAJARITO LAND GRANT
(1685-1746)

Josefa Baca, a descendant of colonists arriving in 1600, acquired the Sitio de San Ysidro de Pajarito, which included a hacienda and large tract of land south of present-day Albuquerque. Establishing a ranch with 950 head of sheep, horses, cattle, and goats with her livestock brand, Josefa became the progenitor of generations of New Mexicans. The village of Pajarito developed around the Baca family compound.

Josefa's son Antonio, sold the Pajarito tract, to Clemente Gutiérrez. His heirs sought confirmation of their claim to the land from the surveyor general in 1877. The Court of Private Land Claims, on the presumption that a grant had been made to Josefa Baca, confirmed the Pajarito Land Grant in 1894 and patented it in 1914. Five generations after Josefa's death, her land and ranch remained within the same family, passing to a fifth great-granddaughter and direct descendant, Juliana Gutiérrez, wife of James Hubbell. The hacienda, lands, acequias, and orchards that survive today are a testament to the family's prosperity.

The petitioners claimed to own the tract because of Spain's grant to Josefa Baca sometime before 1746, as evidenced by her last will and testament.

The Pajarito community is located just outside of Albuquerque, located between the South Valley communities of Los Padillas to the south and Atrisco to the north.

Installation Site

In Pajarito – near the Gutierrez Hubbell House - 6029 Isleta Boulevard, SW

CROSSROADS AT MARTINEZTOWN

Martineztown is at the crossroads of El Camino Real de Tierra Adentro and Tijeras Canyon Trail, two important trade routes begun by Native Americans. The trail through Tijeras Canyon linked the Rio Grande Valley to the plains east of the Sandia Mountains, while the Camino Real primarily followed the river and became the Spanish trade route that brought European culture here beginning in 1598. Edith Boulevard follows the Camino Real and Dr. Martin Luther King, Jr. Avenue, the Tijeras Canyon Trail. Today's Martineztown was a paraje, a stopping off point for travelers on both trails, and still is a place where community, commerce, and culture come together.

Martineztown is one of the oldest neighborhoods in Albuquerque. It is located between two major trade routes started by Native Americans.

The sculpture Southwest Pieta, by the artist, Luis Jimenez, Jr. can be found here. First Lady, Hillary Clinton, designated the sculpture a National Historic Treasure, during her "Save America's Treasure" tour.

Installation Site
Near the intersection of Edith and
Dr. Martin Luther King Jr. Avenue
at Martineztown Park and Longfellow School

· Catron County ·

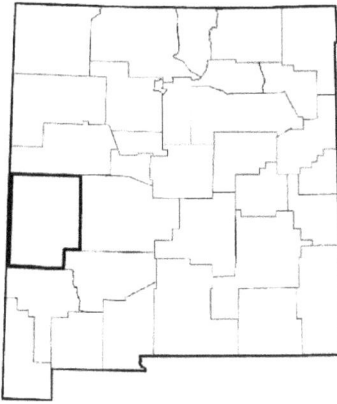

Catron County was named for New Mexico's first U.S. Senator and famous Santa Fe Attorney, Thomas B. Catron. It is the largest county in New Mexico, created February 25, 1921.

County Seat: Reserve

Communities: Luna, Quemado, Datil, Glenwood and Mogollon

6,898 Square Miles

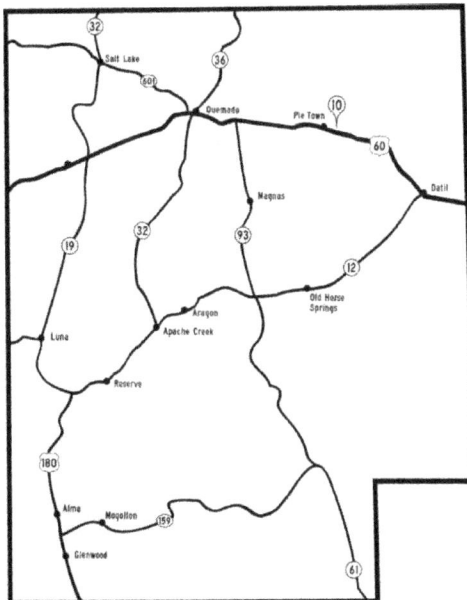

AGNES MORLEY CLEAVELAND
(1874 – 1958)

A native New Mexican, Agnes Morley Cleaveland grew up on her the family's ranch near Datil, New Mexico. Her prize-winning book, <u>No Life for a Lady</u> (1941), is an autobiographical story of a woman's life on a turn-of-the-century ranch. She was educated and lived in other parts of the country, but always returned home to Datil where she spent the last years of her life.

Agnes Morley's family settled near Datil, New Mexico, where Agnes' father built a ranch called the "White House of Datil Canyon." The family later moved into the town of Datil. Her parents sent her to Philadelphia for her education. She lived most of her adulthood outside of New Mexico, becoming a well-known author, journalist, public speaker and women's club organizer. She had four children including her son, Norman Cleaveland, who became a well-known writer of New Mexico history. Agnes spent the last few years of her life on a ranch outside Datil, near her sister Lorraine, a prominent figure in the Datil community.

Installation Site
On NM 60 at Mile Marker 69.5

· Chaves County ·

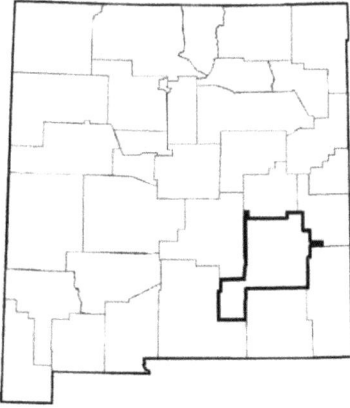

Chaves County was created in 1889 and named for Col. Jose Francisco Chaves, a native of Bernalillo and delegate to Congress.

County Seat: Roswell

Communities: Lake Arthur, Hagerman, Dexter, Mesa and Elkins

6,095 Square Miles

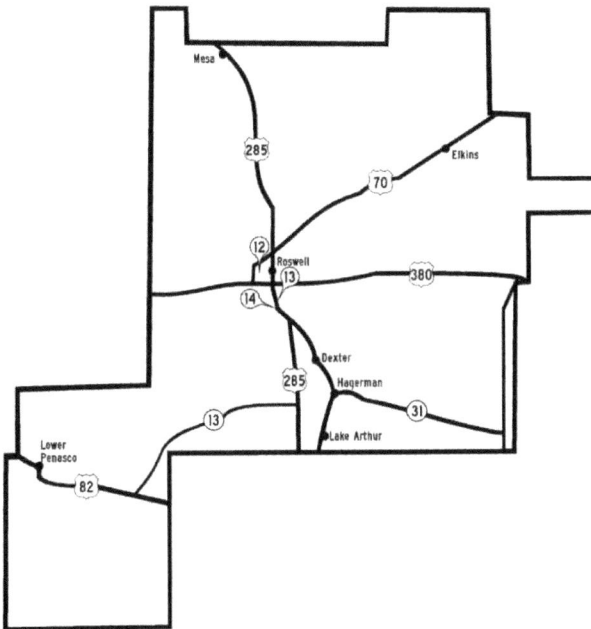

ATLAS MISSILE SILOS

During the Cold War (1946-1989), this area became home for twelve Atlas missile silo sites – America's first operational Intercontinental Ballistic Missile system. They protected the Strategic Air Command facilities at Walker Air Force Base south of Roswell. Due to problems with the Atlas missile, these sites were deactivated in 1965 shortly before the closure of Walker AFB. The abandoned silos are now privately owned.

There are twelve missile silos located in the Roswell area. An interesting fact is that the missiles had to be fueled but could not be launched within the silo. They were raised to the surface for blast off. One of the Cold War Relic Atlas F Missile Silo/Bunker located near Roswell, is now offered as an overnight accommodation through Airbnb.

Installation Site
U.S. 70 at the rest stop
at mile marker 314

THE ROSWELL INCIDENT

Events on a nearby farm in early July 1947 spawned international attention on Roswell, located 85 miles to the southeast. William W. Brazel, a foreman on the J.B. Foster Ranch, found strange material scattered over the farm. Unable to identify the debris, Brazel called the local sheriff, who turned it over to the Roswell Army Air Field. Military officials announced that the debris was the wreckage of a "flying disk." The July 8th front page headline of the Roswell Daily Record read "RAAF Captures Flying Saucer on Ranch in Roswell Region."

The following day, a military official described the incident as a crashed weather balloon. The changing statements captivated the public's imagination, and newspapers worldwide reported on the story. The public's fascination with UFOs continued with the rise of the Atomic Age and space travel in the 1950s and 1960s. Pop culture in the 1980s renewed public interest in UFOS and the "Roswell Incident." Roswell has since become a tourist destination with an annual July UFO Festival.

The Roswell Incident has gone down in history as the most significant UFO encounter of our century, but the facts about the incident remain covered in secrecy.

Installation Site
East from Corona on NM 247, just past Mile Marker 17 near the turnoff to Corona Compressor Station

ROSWELL PRISONER OF WAR CAMP

Camp Roswell was one of the first and largest base camps built in the U.S. and was located on Orchard Park Road. The camp operated from August 1942 to February 1946 and interned 4,816 German POWs at its peak. Camp construction was similar to Army training centers with the addition of watchtowers and fences. Most POWs performed agricultural labor, particularly during cotton season. Associated smaller side camps were located in Fort Sumner, Artesia, and Dexter.

During World War II, 155 prisoners of war (POW) base camps and 511 branch camps were constructed in 46 states. By 1945, over 425,000 German, Italian, and Japanese POWs were held in the U.S., including more than 371,000 Germans. POWs worked in farms, mills, canneries, public works projects, and other low-risk jobs that alleviated labor shortages during the war. New Mexico's larger camps were located in Albuquerque, Las Cruces, Lordsburg, Roswell, and Santa Fe.

At Roswell's POW/MIA Park, the Riverbank Stone Flood Wall features a German iron cross made in 1943 by POWs held nearby in one of the camps.

Installation Site
Intersection of Orchard Park Road and US 285

WALKER AIR FORCE BASE
1941-1967

Roswell Army Air Field was established in1941 and renamed after New Mexico native Brigadier General Kenneth Walker in 1948. Once the Strategic Air Command's largest base, its bomber fleet and Atlas missiles were key deterrents during the early years of the Cold War. WAFB closed in 1967 and became the Roswell International Air Center, home to public and private entities. Two world record free-fall parachute jumps took place here, including Alan Eustace's 135,890-foot descent, which reached a speed of 822 miles per hour, in 2014.

Walker Air Force Base and the Army Air Corps Flying School, located south of the business district of Roswell, New Mexico, opened in 1941.

It was active during World War II and, after the war, became known as Roswell Army Airfield. The Air Force Base closed in 1967.

Installation Site
West side of US 285 in Roswell
near Hobson Road exit

· Cibola County ·

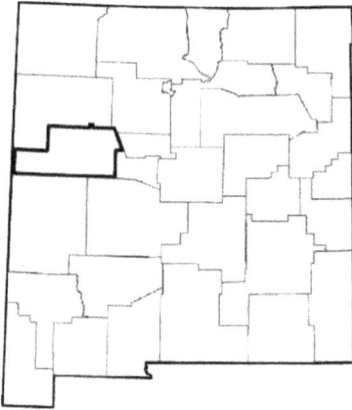

Named for the Cibola National Forest, Cibola County is New Mexico's newest county created in 1981.

County Seat: Grants

Communities: Milan, Fenton Lake, Laguna and Seboyeta

4,180 Square Miles

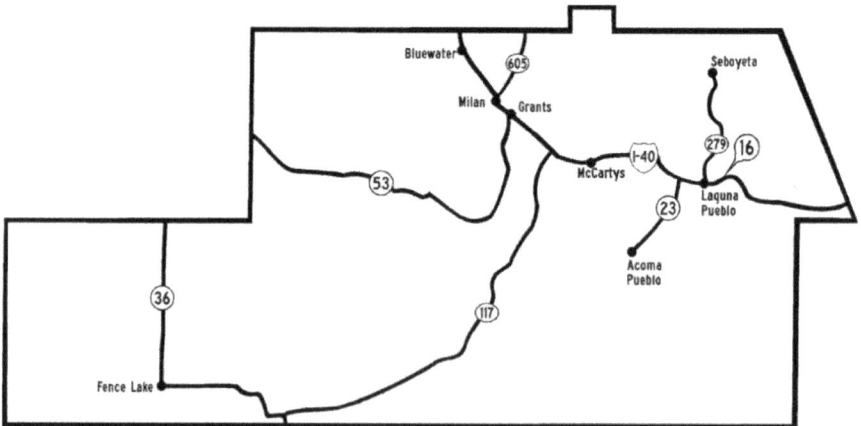

SUSIE RAYOS MARMON
GA-WA GOO MAN (EARLY RISER)
1877 – 1988

Educated at the Carlisle Indian School in Pennsylvania under the U.S. policy of acculturating Indian children through schooling and removal from their homelands, Susie was instrumental in bringing education back to Laguna. A lifelong teacher, oral historian, and storyteller, Susie was honored with a school in her name in Albuquerque in 1989 and received many national and state citations for her commitment to educating students.

Susie was called Ga-wa goo man, which means "early riser." She devoted her life to her family and her career as an educator of Indian children. It was rare for an Indian girl to pursue higher education at the turn of the 20th century, and Susie graduated from Bloomsburg State Teacher's College in Pennsylvania in 1906. She and her husband, Walter Marmon, raised their children at the Laguna Pueblo, where Susie taught the Pueblo children in a one-room building behind her home in Laguna for nearly fifty years.

An oral historian, Susie told Laguna stories of legends in that classroom over one hundred years ago. Those important legends are being told today in the school in Albuquerque that bears her name, serving to inspire students of various heritages.

Susie's dedication and accomplishments in education reflect the high value the Laguna people put on the importance of education. Ahead of her time, her life story exemplified the blending of two cultures, retaining the old while learning the new.

Installation Site
US 70 at Mile Marker 256.2, west of Albuquerque

· Colfax County ·

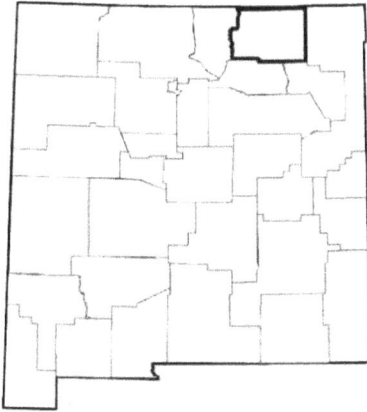

Colfax County has four communities that have been the County Seat during its long and colorful history.

County Seat: Raton

Communities: Angel Fire, Eagle Nest, Cimarron and Springer

3,768 Square Miles

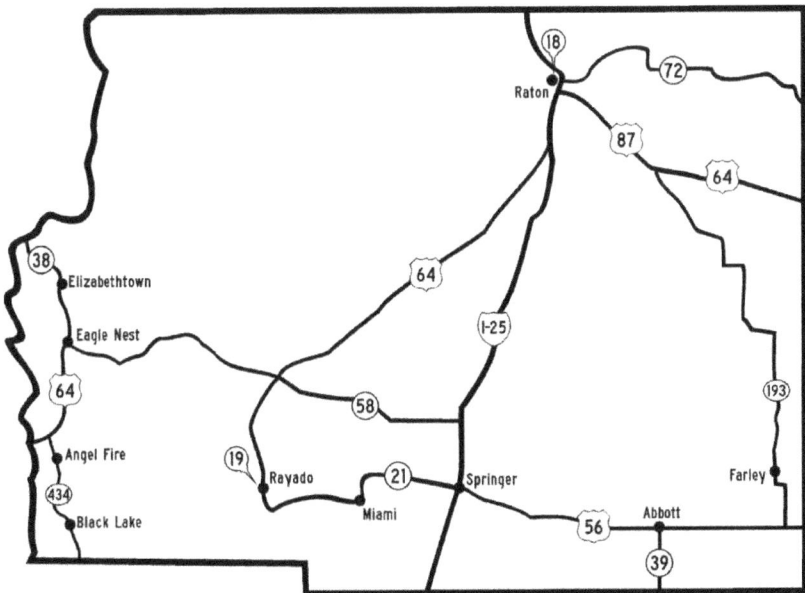

FIRST AUTOMOBILE IN NEW MEXICO

Robert L. Dodson bought a steam-powered Locomobile in Denver with plans to drive it to Albuquerque. Accompanied by a Locomobile representative, on November 30, 1900, the pair became the first motorists to traverse treacherous Raton Pass into New Mexico. The trip to Raton, largely on wagon roads, took five days. A few days later the Locomobile arrived in Albuquerque to fanfare and some consternation.

According to the press reports at the time, the City of Albuquerque greeted the Locomobile with excitement and fear. Because the Locomobile scared horses, the city had considered banning it. Over time, however, it became the preferred mode of transportation.

Installation Site
NM 87164, State Visitor Information Center at Raton
I-25 exit 451

MARÍA DE LA LUZ BEAUBIEN MAXWELL (1829-1900) MAXWELL LAND GRANT

María de la Luz Beaubien, age 13, wed fur-trapper Lucien Maxwell in 1844, forever linking her to the history of the Maxwell Land Grant and New Mexico. She was born in 1829 to Charles H. Beaubien and María Pabla Lobato. Upon the death of her father in 1864, she inherited a share of her father's portion of the Beaubien-Miranda Land Grant. Luz and her husband purchased the remaining Beaubien parcels as well as the Miranda lands, thereby owning the entire expansive tract that became known as the Maxwell Land Grant.

The Maxwell Land Grant was the largest privately owned contiguous tract of land in the United States, comprising 1,714,765 acres in northeaster New Mexico and southern Colorado. It originated from the 1841 Beaubien-Miranda Land Grant that Governor Manuel Armijo made to Charles Beaubien and Guadalupe Miranda. After Beaubien's death in 1864, his son-in-law, Lucien Maxwell, and daughter, María de la Luz, acquired the grant through inheritance and purchase. Maxwell was one of the wealthiest and most powerful men in New Mexico. The Maxwells sold the land to an English company in 1870. Later disputes between settlers and grant owners characterized the history of northeastern New Mexico in the late 19th century and precipitated the Colfax County War.

When María de la Luz Beaubien married fur-trapper Lucien Maxwell in 1844, the headlines read "Taos Heiress Marries Mountain Man." By 1864, he had become one of the wealthiest and most powerful men in New Mexico.

Installation Site
NM 21 in Rayado, near the Kit Carson Museum

· Curry County ·

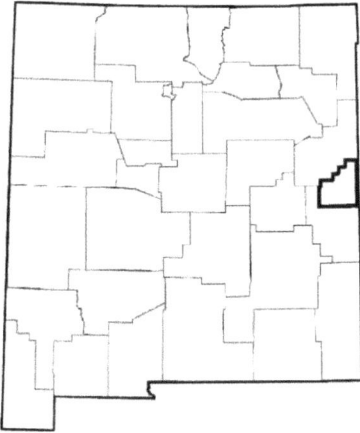

George Curry, a Kansas native who was territorial governor of New Mexico from 1907-1910, helped to create Curry County in 1909.

County Seat: Clovis

Communities: Grady, Texico, Melrose and Bellview

1,404 Square Miles

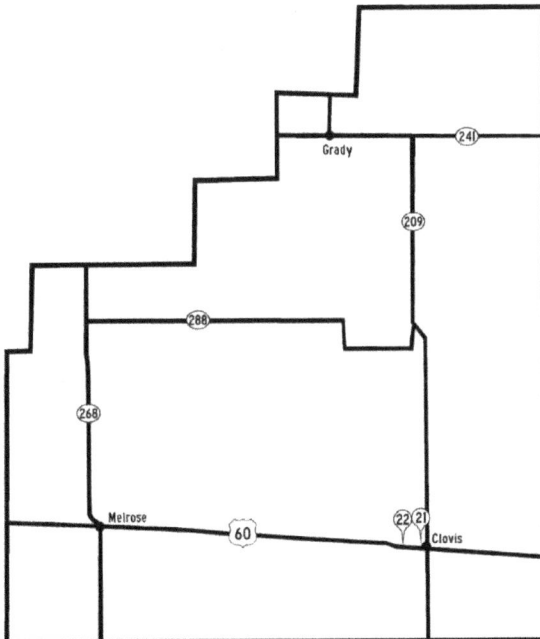

LINCOLN-JACKSON SCHOOL

The African-American Community of Clovis started its first school, Lincoln-Jackson in 1924 with two students. In 1926, the school was named for Ida Jackson, a favorite teacher, and Abraham Lincoln. By 1954, K-12 enrollment had reached 292 students. After the Supreme Court's Desegregation Decision in 1954, the school board eliminated Lincoln-Jackson High School. In 1966 it became Lincoln-Jackson Elementary, and is now a magnet school for the arts.

In 2017, the Lincoln Jackson School was placed on the National Register of Historic Places. Lincoln-Jackson Elementary School became a magnet school for the arts called the Lincoln-Jackson Art Academy. Then in 2019, the school was renamed the iAcademy at Lincoln Jackson, providing both academic and creative curriculum to grades second through twelfth.

Installation Site
On the north side of the Lincoln-Jackson School on NM 60/84, Alton Street in Clovis

NORMAN PETTY

At thirteen, Norman began cutting records in his father's filling station. With money earned from the Norman Petty Trio's "Mood Indigo." Petty converted a family grocery store next door into a modern recording studio where he experimented with echo and microphone settings. In 1957, Petty made rock'n'roll history recording Buddy Holly and the Crickets' "That'll Be the Day." The sound influenced a generation.

Many great artists like Roy Orbison, Waylon Jennings, and Buddy Holly, among other well-known musicians, have recorded at Norman Petty Studios. *The King of Clovis*, a book about Petty by Frank Blanas, was published in 2014.

Installation Site
Near the Norman Petty Studios –
1313 W. Seventh Street, Clovis

· **DeBaca County** ·

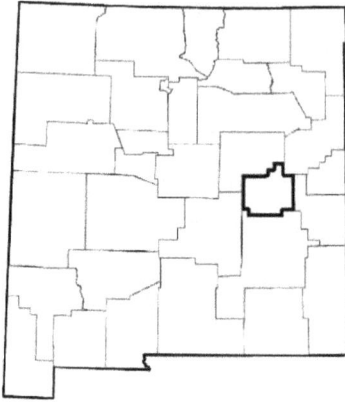

DeBaca County was created in 1917 and named for Ezequiel Cabeza de Baca, New Mexico's second governor.

County Seat: Fort Sumner

Communities: Tiaba and Yeso

2,366 Square Miles

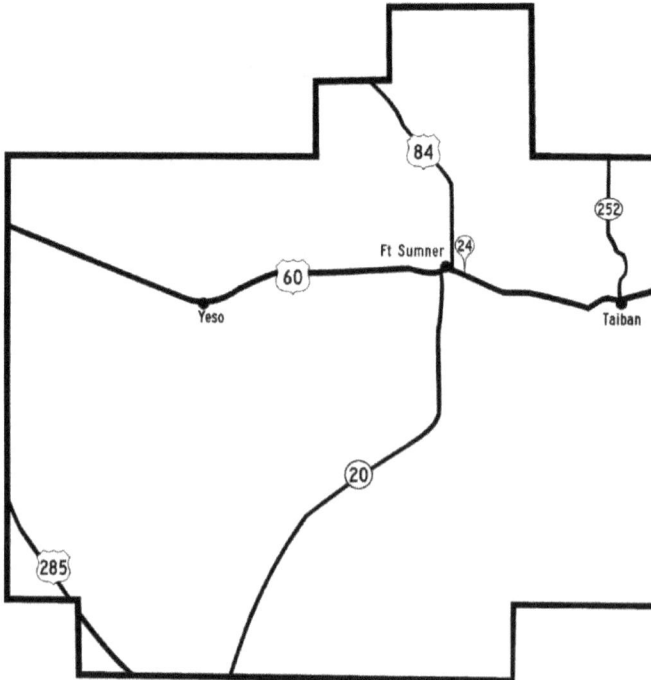

HELENE HAACK ALLEN
(1891 – 1978)

Helene was a pioneer businesswoman, moving to Fort Sumner at 21. She married a homesteader and they ran diverse businesses, including theaters and a mortuary. She established the first Billy the Kid museum on the site of the Old Fort and won legal battles to keep him interred there. Late in life, she donated land, which became Fort Sumner State Monument and Bosque Redondo Memorial Museum.

Helene married John Allen, a homesteader, on January 29, 1913.

Together they managed local theaters, a farm at the site of the old Fort Sumner, a mortuary, and the graveyard where Billy the Kid is buried. When John died in 1945, Helene continued her work to establish the first Billy the Kid Museum. Billy the Kid was killed in Fort Sumner in 1881.

She is best known for donating fifty acres to the State Land Office, which the Commissioner of Public Lands, Guyton B. Hayes in 1968 declared it a state monument. This monument recognized the centennial year of the Treaty of 1868 on May 17, 1968, and President Lyndon Johnson issued a proclamation in honor of the treaty at its 100th anniversary of the original signing.

Installation Site
US 60 at Mile Marker 330.8 - Fort Sumner

· Doña Ana County ·

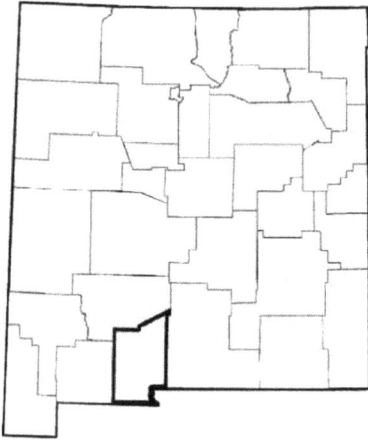

Doña Ana County is reputed to be named for a Doña Ana Robledo, renowned for her charitable acts in the 17th Century. It was created on January 9, 1852.

County Seat: Las Cruces

Communities: Anthony, La Mesa, Mesilla, Organ, Radium Springs, Leasburg and Hatch

2,366 Square Miles

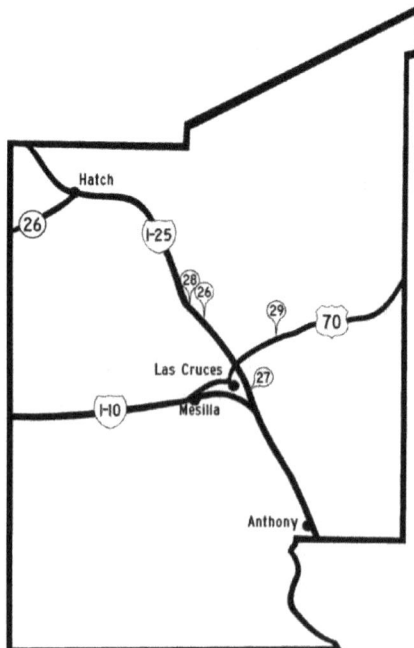

JORNADA DEL MUERTO

This stretch of the Camino Real leaves the Rio Grande and cuts across 90 miles of desert with little water or shelter. Despite the challenges it presented, Spanish, Mexican, and Anglo travelers between El Paso and the settlements in northern New Mexico heavily used the dreaded "Deadman's Journey." On horseback, travelers could cross the Jornada in a few days, but people on foot accompanying ox-drawn carts or wagons could spend a week in transit.

Jornada del Muerto is translated loosely from Spanish, historically referring to it as the "Single Day's Journey of the Dead Man." It referred to a dry 100-mile trail between Socorro and Las Cruces.

Installation Site
I-25 Southbound Rest Area - Mile Marker 23

MARÍA GUTIÉRREZ SPENCER
(1919 – 1992)

Punished for not speaking English in school, María Gutiérrez Spencer devoted her life to validating the Indo-Hispano experience. A graduate of University of California, Berkeley and New Mexico State University, she pioneered bilingual and bicultural education in New Mexico, founded BOLD: Bicultural Orientation and Language Development in Silver City. Maria battled cancer for 50 years, but traveled worldwide to train teachers. She was honored by the Wonder Woman Foundation with Rosa Parks in 1981.

María Gutiérrez Spencer was born in Las Cruces, New Mexico, December 17, 1919 to Jesús Borunda Gutiérrez and Aurora Valdéz Gutiérrez.

Although she could not speak English when she began her education in a Catholic primary school, she graduated from high school as the class salutatorian. She received her bachelor's degree in Linguistics from the University of California at Berkeley. In addition, she completed a master's degree in Spanish from New Mexico State University.

She began teaching bilingual education in the Las Cruces schools, and by this time, she was married to Lewis Spenser, a professor of music, and had two daughters. She was one of the first teachers in the country to develop a separate curriculum for native speakers of Spanish for Las Cruces High School. Ultimately her curriculum was converted into a teacher training program, and Maria retired and continued working as a social activist until she died in 1992.

Her daughter Laura Gutierrez-Spencer also had a successful career in education. After seven years on the University of Nevada, Las Vegas faculty, Gutierrez-Spencer returned to Las Cruces to lead Chicano Programs in 1996. She also worked on the Danny Villanueva scholarship program.

Installation Site
New Mexico State University campus
in Las Cruces on Espina Street - NM 138 between E.
University Avenue and Stewart Street

PARAJE SAN DIEGO

This paraje, or stopping place, was one of the most important on the entire length of the Camino Real. It provided travelers with a final opportunity to water their stock, taking them down Tonuco Draw to the river, and to prepare their caravans before leaving the Rio Grande Valley and entering the desolate Jornada del Muerto. Journeyers on their way to Santa Fe started in the evening and traveled non-stop until they reached the Paraje de Fra Cristóbal 100 miles to the north. People headed south faced a day's journey to Paraje Robledo near the site of Ft. Selden.

San Diego Mountain, also known as Tonuco Mountain, is an American Summit 22 miles northwest of Las Cruces. It marked the location of the Paraje San Diego, one of the Spanish campsites along the El Camino Real.

This area is well known for its challenging Jeep trail, petroglyphs, mining, and the Camino Real. In 1927, Congress granted the areas surrounding Tonuco Mountain to New Mexico State University, and since that point in time, the site has become known as the "College Ranch."

Installation Site
I-25 Southbound Rest Area, Mile Marker 27

SITE OF SAN AGUSTIN SPRINGS

Here on July 27, 1861, a small force of Confederate soldiers from Colonel John R. Baylor's Second Texas Mounted Rifles overtook straggling Union troops of the Seventh Infantry who had suffered defeat in a skirmish at Mesilla two days earlier. Many Union soldiers had unwisely filled their canteens with medicinal whiskey rather than water for their retreat from Fort Fillmore to Fort Stanton. Dehydrated and exhausted from the heat and in desperate need of water, the Union troops attempted to cross the Organ Mountains through the pass and were intercepted at the spring. Unable to fight, Major Isaac Lynde surrendered his command without firing a single shot over the vigorous protest of his officers.

San Agustin Spring, formerly known as San Augustine Springs, is a spring in the Organ Mountains located in Doña Ana County, New Mexico. During the Early American Civil War, this spring was the famous site of a humiliating surrender of Union Army forces to the Confederates.

Installation Site
US 70 at Mile Marker 162.9 - East of Las Cruces

· **Eddy County** ·

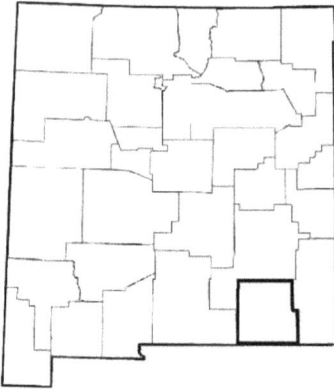

Created in 1889, Eddy County was named for the developer who brought the railroad to the area, Charles B. Eddy.

County Seat: Las Cruces

Communities: Anthony, La Mesa, Mesilla, Organ, Radium Springs, Leasburg and Hatch

4,180 Square Miles

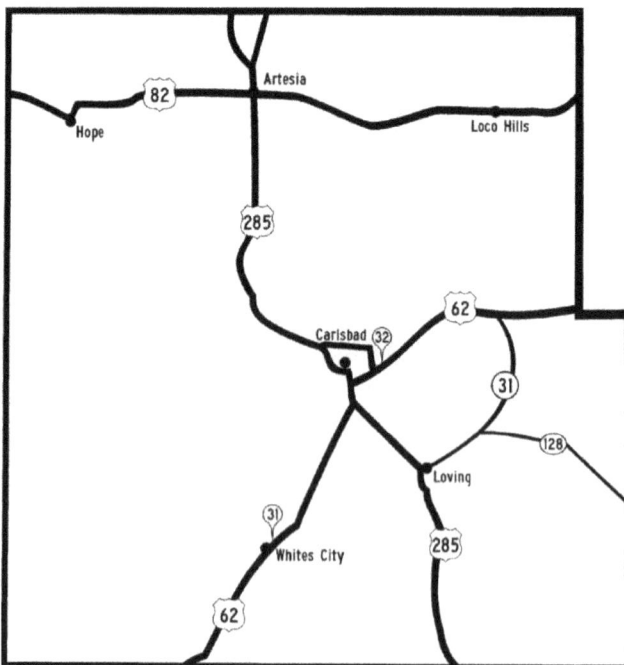

CARLSBAD CAVERNS
NATIONAL PARK

These vast magnificent caverns contain over 21 miles of explored corridors. The chambers have countless stalactites and stalagmites unrivaled in size and beauty. The caverns are within a reef that formed in an ancient sea 240 million years ago. Millions of years later, the reef was fractured, allowing ground water to begin work fashioning the cavern. The caverns became a National Monument in 1923, a National Park in 1930 and a World Heritage property in 1995.

Carlsbad Caverns National Park is in the Chihuahuan Desert of southern New Mexico, over 1,000 feet deep, and contains over 100 limestone caves and 30 miles of mapped passages. The Carlsbad Cavern is the largest easily accessible cave in North America.

Installation Site
US 62/180, Mile Marker 15.25_in Carlsbad

POTASH DISCOVERY AT McSWEENEY – McNUTT

The World War I embargo on the importation of German potash spurred exploratory drilling in the United States. In 1925, while drilling for petroleum, geologist Vachel Harry McNutt discovered a vast deposit of potash ores. Located one mile south of here, the McSweeny – McNutt #1 discovery ended the nation's dependence on imported potash and created a new industry in southeastern New Mexico. Commercial potash mining began in 1926 with the incorporation of the American Potash Company, and since then over 248-million tons of ore has been mined from the Carlsbad area.

Potash is the common term for mined and manufactured salts containing the element potassium in a water-soluble form. Historically, potash was made from residue left by the evaporation of water-soaked wood ash and used for manufacturing soap, textiles, and glass. Potash in the form of potassium chloride and potassium carbonate is used in fertilizers. New Mexico's Permian Basin has the largest concentration of potash ores in the United States.

Vachel McNutt who lived from 1888 to 1936, is known for discovering the first commercial potash deposits in the Western Hemisphere. He was also known as a accomplished petroleum geologist.

Installation Site
US Route 62/180 East of Carlsbad - South side of highway - Mile Marker 58/59

· **Grant County** ·

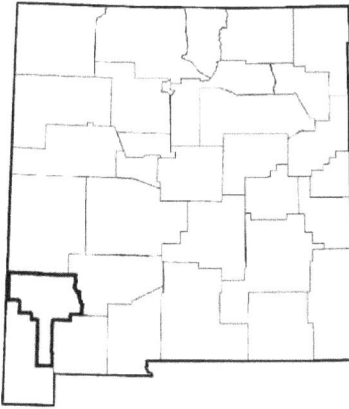

The name "Grant" honors the great General and U.S. President, Ulysses S. Grant. This county was created on January 30, 1868.

County Seat: Silver City

Communities: Bayard, Gila, Hachita, Hurley, Cliff, Piños Altos and Santa Rita

3,970 Square Miles

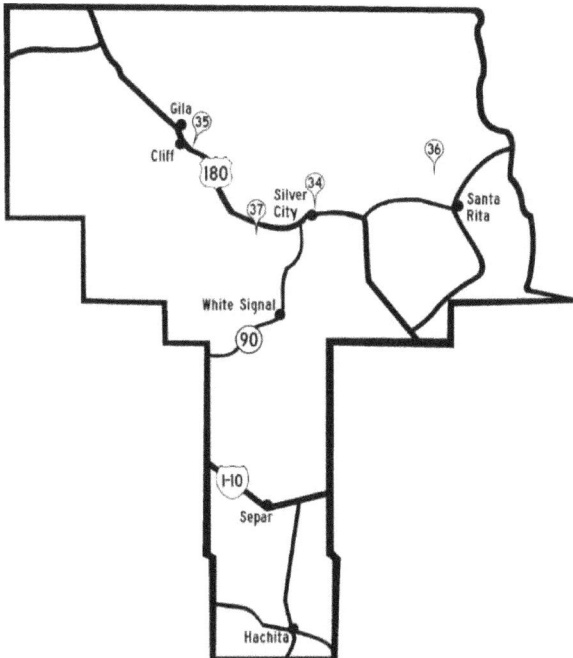

ANITA SCOTT COLEMAN
(1890 – 1960)

Anita Scott Coleman's mother was a slave and her father a Buffalo Soldier. Raised on a ranch near Silver City, her award-winning essays, stories, and poems emphasized racial pride and black women's issues during the Harlem Renaissance, the "New Negro Movement" of the 1920s. Her essay "Arizona and New Mexico – The Land of Esperanza" speaks of opportunity in a land of hope: "For here prevails for every man be he white or black a hardier philosophy – and a bigger and better chance, that is not encountered elsewhere in these United States."

Anita Scott Coleman studied at New Mexico Teachers College in Silver City. Her teaching career ended in 1916 when she married James Harold Coleman, a printer and photographer born in Virginia.

Coleman published stories, essays, and poems in many national magazines during the 1920s and 1930s. Several of the periodicals were major outlets for Harlem Renaissance writers. During her lifetime, she published more than 30 short stories. Her work became well-known as the Harlem Renaissance emerged. Her children's book, The Singing Bells, was published after her death in 1961.

Installation Site

Intersection of NM 90 and Broadway at Murray Ryan Visitor Center in Silver City

GILA, NEW MEXICO LYONS & CAMPBELL RANCH HEADQUARTERS

The one-million-acre L.C. completely overshadowed other ranches in southwestern New Mexico. At peak operation, 60,000 cattle grazed mountains and grasslands stretching to Arizona; 75 cowboys and 100 families ranched and farmed the land from the 1880's until 1917. Englishman Tom Lyons and prospector Angus Campbell created an empire that was one of the truly great ranches of the West. Lyons built a lavish home in Gila and a mountain hunting lodge accessible only by pack trail. Landholdings were sold after Lyon's murder in 1917, but his home, ranch headquarters, and Catholic church he built for his family and employees still stand in Gila.

The Lyons Campbell Ranch headquarters is rich in history dating back to 1810, and was the "company town" of the cattle operation, which consisted of a herd of 60,000 cattle. The main house accommodated about 75 cowboys. There were bunkhouses, a saloon, post office, chapel, jail, theater, and an adobe mansion for Tom and Ida Lyons.

Installation Site
NW corner of intersection at US 180 and
NM Hwy 211

THE DEATH OF MANGAS COLORADAS
JANUARY 18, 1863

Mangas Coloradas was one of the most highly regarded leaders among the Chiricahua Apaches. Born in 1795, he was noted for his sagacity, diplomacy, and at 6'6" his height. He met with U.S. General Kearny in 1846 and in 1852 negotiated the only approved treaty between the Chiricahua tribe and the United States. During attempted peace talks in 1862, he was arrested and taken to Fort McLane, which stood near this site, where he was tortured and shot by guards. His skull was sent back East never to be recovered.

Apache Chief Mangas Coloradas lived from 1793 to 1863 and was known as a skilled war leader against both the Mexicans and the Americans. Historians consider him one of the most important Native American leaders of the 19th century.

Installation Site
US 182 near Mile Marker 132 on the
east side of the highway

MIMBRES VALLEY

People have lived in the Mimbres Valley since at least 2000 B.C. and probably earlier. Small villages of farmers lived in pit houses – underground single-family structures – by A.D. 200. Around A.D.1000, people began erecting pueblos, similar to the one at nearby Mattocks Ruin, that housed up to 200 people. The Mimbreños are best known for their exquisite black-on-white painted pottery decorated with humans, animals, and intricate geometric designs, one of the most spectacular artistic traditions of the ancient New World. Later groups built smaller villages after A.D.1130, but Pueblo peoples left the region by A.D. 1450. The last indigenous occupants were Apaches who lived here through the late 1800's.

The Mimbres Valley American Viticultural Area (AVA) is located in southwestern New Mexico near the towns of Deming and Silver City. It covers 636,000 acres of semi-desert and 2,000 acres of grape vines for winemaking. The land is similar to the Mendoza winemaking region of Argentina.

Installation Site
NM 35 near intersection of Sage
Drive in Mimbres

· Guadalupe County ·

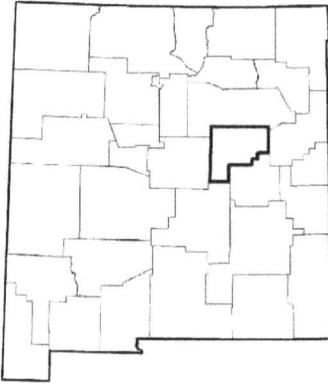

Guadalupe County was created by the territorial legislature of 1891. The name honors Our Lady of Guadalupe, the vision of the Virgin Mary that appeared to Juan Diego near Mexico City in 1531.

County Seat: Santa Rosa

Communities: Cuervo, Newkirk, Colonias, Anton Chico, Milagro, Pastura, Puerto de Luna and Vaughn

2,999 Square Miles

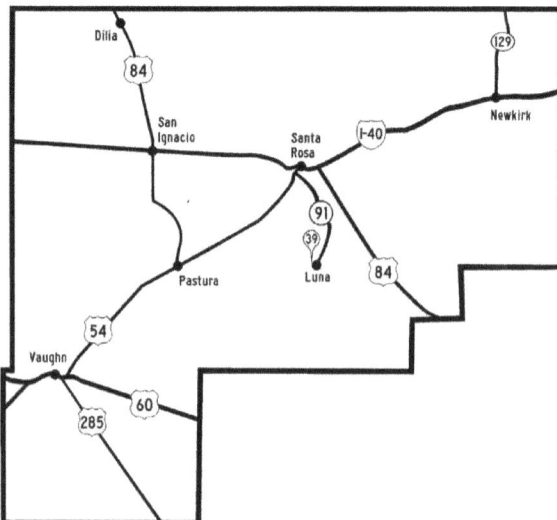

VÁSQUEZ DE CORONADO'S ROUTE

In May 1541, Spanish explorer Francisco Vásquez de Coronado halted his expedition along the west bank of the Pecos River for four days while they built a bridge across the river. The expedition then spent the next several months searching for the fabled riches of Quivera in the plains of Texas, Oklahoma, and Kansas. In early 1542, the disillusioned explorers returned through here on their way back to Mexico.

The Spanish explorer Francisco Vásquez de Coronado, who lived from 1510 to 1554, was serving as Governor of an important province in New Spain (Mexico) when he heard reports of the alleged Seven Golden Cities located to the north of what later became the southwestern region of the United States. Because he did not find these cities, the expedition was considered a failure.

Installation Site
NM 91 at the Puerto de Luna Senior
Citizens Center

· Harding County ·

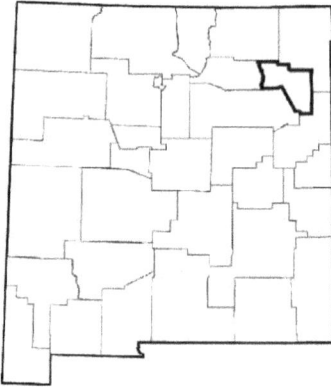

This county was created by the state legislature on March, 4, 1921, the same day Warren G. Harding was inaugurated 29th President of the United States.

County Seat: Mosquero

Communities: Roy

2,125 Square Miles

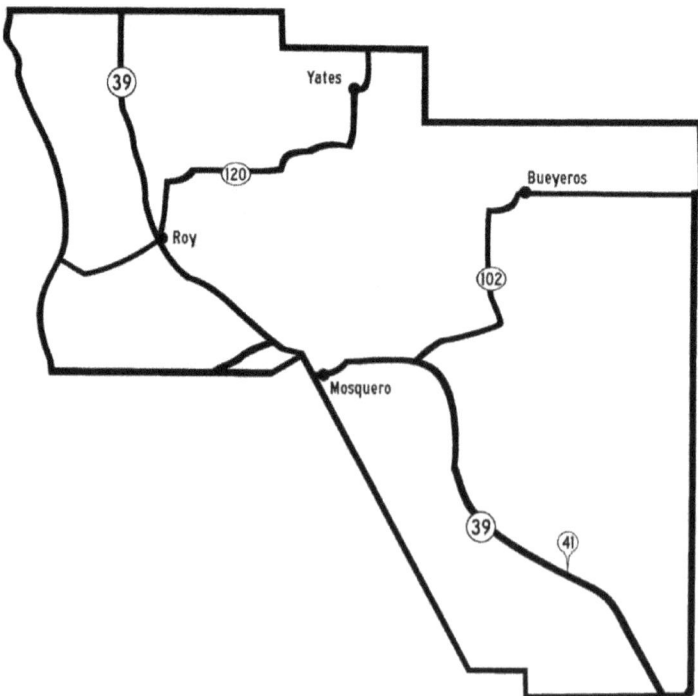

MONICA GALLEGOS
(1851 – 1909)
CARLOTTA GALLEGOS
(1857 – 1936)

Monica and Carlotta Gallegos, widowed sister, ranched 375,000 acres. Monica operated a general store and saloon and issued scrip in her name. When Black Jack Ketchum raided the ranch in 1890, Monica shot him in the arm. The sisters built a school and, in 1876, the Church of the Immaculate Conception, furnished with large Italian statues. Their vision ensured economic and social stability in Gallegos.

Monica and Carlotta were ranchers and entrepreneurs with business enterprises which helped to create the community of Gallegos. Monica operated a general store and a saloon and issued scrip, a form of certified money written from a company or bank and usable in that same company or bank. They also were known for having built a school for the children in the community. The church that they built in 1876 was replaced in 1914 with the form you will see on a visit to the town today.

Installation Site
NM 39, Exit 278 east of Albuquerque

· Hidalgo County ·

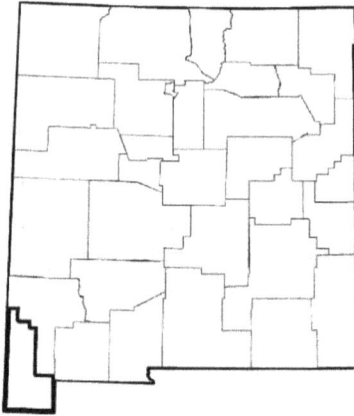

Hidalgo County was named for the Mexican town of Guadalupe Hidalgo, where the Guadalupe-Hidalgo treaty was signed in1848. The county was created on February 25, 1919.

County Seat: Lordsburg

Communities: Antelope Wells, Rodeo, Animas, Cotton City and Virden

3,447 Square Miles

THE WOMEN OF SHAKESPEARE
EMMA MARBLE MUIR
(1873 – 1959)
RITA WELLS HILL
(1901 – 1985)
JANALOO HILL HOUGH
(1939 – 2005)

Three remarkable women devoted much of their lives to preserving Shakespeare. When aged nine, Emma Marble Muir's parents moved to the prosperous mining town where she learned its quirky history from "Uncle" Johnny Evenson, the stage keeper. In 1935, Rita Wells Hill, a silent-film actress, purchased the ghost town and surrounding ranchlands with her husband Frank. They began restoring Shakespeare, and moved into the mercantile, where they raised their daughter, Janaloo.

Emma appeared one day on horseback at the Hill's property, friendship followed and she shared the town's history with Rita and in stories she wrote for New Mexico Magazine. Rita and Janaloo from their own research wrote prolifically about the town, which became a tourist draw. Until their deaths, Rita and Janaloo worked tirelessly to showcase Shakespeare as an authentic ghost town and to preserve the ranching way of life.

Emma Marble Muir arrived at the mining town of Shakespeare in 1882. She and her daughter, Rita Wells Muir, learned to appreciate and preserve the town's history. Rita and her husband bought Shakespeare as part of their ranch in 1935. Rita passed the ranch to her daughter, Janaloo Hill Hough.

Janaloo and her husband continued fighting for the history and preservation of Shakespeare. Investing their own resources, they rebuilt some of the buildings destroyed by fire in 1997. Without the dedication of this mother, daughter, and granddaughter, the ghost town of Shakespeare would not exist today.

Installation Site
NM 180 - Exit 41 – Follow the
Signs to Lordsburg

· **Lea County** ·

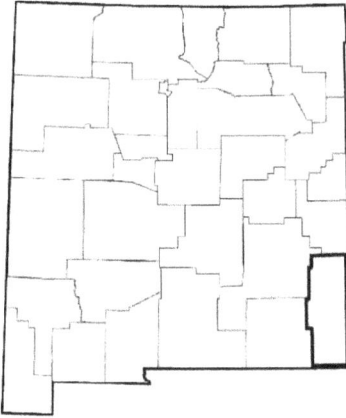

Captain Joseph Calloway Lea, a prominent leader in Chaves County and founder of the New Mexico Military Academy, was honored by having Lea County named after him in 1917.

County Seat: Lovington

Communities: Caprock, Tatum McDonald, Jal, Buckeye, Oil Center, Eunice, Maljama and Bennett

4,394 Square Miles

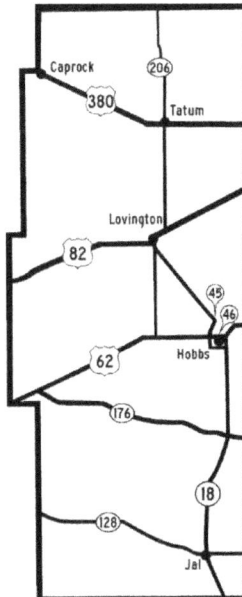

HOBBS ARMY AIRFIELD

Built in 1942, the Hobbs Army Airfield was primarily used to train pilots to operate B-17 Bomber planes. It was built for the U.S. Army Air Forces 50,000 Pilot Training Program and closed in 1948. In 2003 it became Hobbs Industrial Airpark and was used for glider operations. The Harry McAdams Park, Ocotillo Golf Course and New Mexico Junior College now cover much of the base.

Hobbs Army Airfield was used during World War II by the United States Army Air Forces Air Training Command as part of the Western Fight Training Center, located near Hobbs, New Mexico.

Installation Site
Highway 18 at Ocotillo Park in Hobbs

HOBBS DISCOVERY WELL

Following earlier oil discoveries in the Lea County area, Ronald K. DeFord, of Midwest Refining Co., now Amoco, came to Hobbs to survey for a new drilling site. Drilling began October 12, 1927, oil was discovered at 4,065 feet, and the new well produced over 500,000 barrels of oil in its lifetime. Hobbs was transformed from an unknown community into a bustling boomtown boasting many restaurants and bars, several hotels and move theaters.

In 1928, the discovery of an oil well brought wealth to Lea County and the town of Hobbs, named for James Hobbs, who homesteaded there. The Hobbs discovery came nearly six years after the first oil production, and at the time, it quickly became known as the most critical single oil find in New Mexico's history.

Installation Site
US 62 and Grimes Street in Hobbs

· **Lincoln County** ·

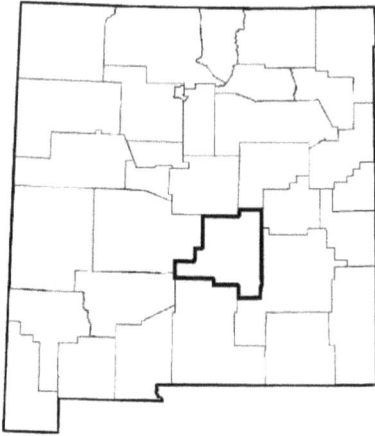

Lincoln County was created by the territorial legislature of 1869, named in honor of President Abraham Lincoln.

County Seat: Carrizozo

Communities: Ruidoso, Alto, Glencoe, San Patricio, Hondo, Tinnie, Piccacho, Angus, Nogal, White Oaks, Corona and Lincoln

4,859 Square Miles

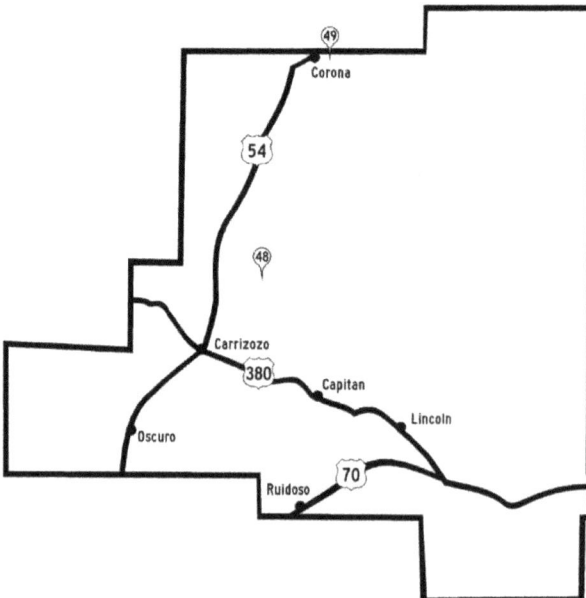

SUSAN McSWEEN BARBER
(1845-1931)
CATTLE QUEEN OF NEW MEXICO

Born Susan Hummer in Gettysburg, Pennsylvania, she married Canadian-born lawyer Alexander McSween. Moving to the New Mexico territory in 1875, the couple figured prominently in the Lincoln County War, joining forces with John Tunstall in opposition to the Dolan-Murphy faction's corrupt cattle business practices. In retaliation, Susan's husband was killed, and her house burned down. She lost a court battle due to the Santa Fe Ring's ties to the faction, but went on to challenge Lawrence Murphy in his own arena – cattle.

Her second husband was George Barber. Under the Desert Land Act, they patented 400 acres in 1883. The act required irrigating the land and in 1881 Susan built a dam across Three Rivers stream and a half-mile ditch to convey water to her property. By 1888 Susan had taken on two partners, claimed ownership of 1,158 acres, and acquired 8,000 head of cattle. The Three Rivers Ranch made her the territory's largest cattle baroness and thus the Cattle Queen of New Mexico. Susan is buried in the White Oaks cemetery.

Susan McSween lived from 1845 to 1931 and became known as the "Cattle Queen of New Mexico." She remarried in 1880 to a young lawyer, George Barber, whom she later divorced. By 1890 she had an 1158-acre ranch, Three Rivers Cattle Company, becoming extremely wealthy through cattle sales and mining a small silver vein on her property. Then in 1902, she sold her ranch holdings and moved to White Oaks, New Mexico, where she lived the rest of her life and is buried in the White Oaks Cemetery

She has been portrayed in several movies about the Lincoln County War, including the 1988 movie, Young Guns.

Installation Site
Near White Oak Cemetery on NM 349

Carrizozo Woman's Club

Woman's clubs play an important role in communities by providing volunteer opportunities, performing civic and social improvements, and establishing public buildings and parks. In New Mexico independent woman's clubs formed in the late 19th and early 20th centuries. The New Mexico Federation of Woman's Clubs was established in 1911 and is affiliated with the national General Federation of Women's Clubs founded in 1890. The Carrizozo Woman's Club was founded in 1920 and is a member of both federations. The club met in public buildings and members' houses before this building was constructed.

The Carrizozo Woman's Club building serves as a gathering place for cultural, community, and social events. The building was constructed in 1939 with Works Progress Administration (WPA) funding and was designed by Jess C. Garrison, a local builder and WPA crew foreman. The building is an excellent example of Pueblo Revival-style architecture with its adobe construction, exposed vigas, and portal. The main meeting room, the Round Room, has elaborate ceiling with exposed vigas radiating from a central point.

The Carrizozo Woman's Club building was placed on the State and National Register of Historic Places in 2003.

Since the club's founding over one hundred years ago, it has taken the lead in bringing sanitation, natural gas, paved streets, and a library to the community. The members have maintained the Evergreen Cemetery,

Spider Park, and Spencer Park in Carrizozo. Annually they spearhead a veteran's celebration and Keep Zozo Clean event, high school scholarship program, among other initiatives.

Installation Site
908 11th Street in Carrizozo

· **Los Alamos County** ·

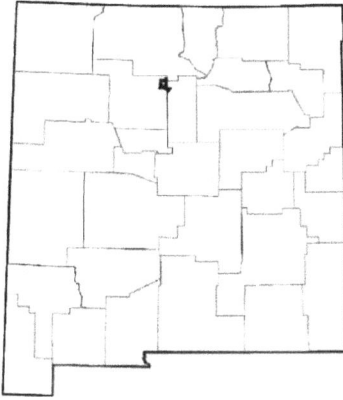

The smallest of New Mexico's counties, Los Alamos was created in 1949 and was named for the town which became its county seat. The National Laboratory located in Los Alamos was once a secret facility whose work helped bring an end to World War II.

County Seat: Los Alamos

Communities: White Rock

4,859 Square Miles

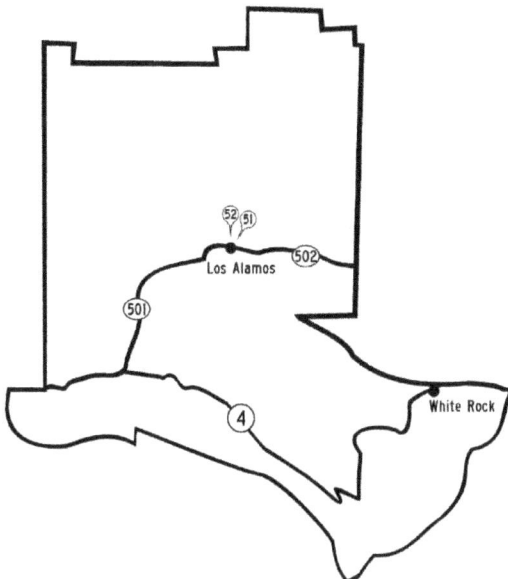

MARJORIE BELL CHAMBERS, Ph.D.
(1923 – 2006)
HISTORIAN AND MENTOR OF WOMEN

Marjorie Bell Chambers advised Governors and Presidents, participated in the formation of the United Nations, and headed two women's colleges. She was president of the Los Alamos Girl Scouts, a founding member of the Historical Society and a project historian of the US Atomic Energy Commission for Los Alamos. She served on the County Council, campaigned for Congress, and traveled worldwide advocating for women's rights.

Marjorie Bell Chambers married William Chambers and raised four children while pursuing an education and eventually receiving her doctorate. She was responsible for advising Governors and Presidents, participated in the formation of the United Nations, and headed two women's colleges.

She was the President of the Los Alamos Girls Scouts, a founding member of the Historical Society, and a Project Historian of the U.S. Atomic Energy Commission for Los Alamos. She served in the County Council, campaigned for Congress, and traveled worldwide, advocating for women's rights.

Installation Site
In the town center of Los Alamos at Ashley Pond

PEGGY POND CHURCH
(1903 – 1986)

Peggy Pond Church, author of the Southwest classic, The House of Otowi Bridge and the daughter of Los Alamos Ranch School Founder, Ashley Pond, will forever be "The First Lady of New Mexican Poetry." As she rode the Pajarito Plateau and camped beneath tall pines, she came to understand that "it is the land that wants to be said." She captured it in her sensitive poems.

She was born in 1903 in Valmora, in the New Mexico Territory. She was the daughter of Ashley Pond Jr. and Hazel Hallett Pond. Her father had been one of Teddy Roosevelt's Rough Riders until he contracted typhoid fever and came to New Mexico to recuperate. While regaining his health, he fell in love with the land and Peggy's mother, the granddaughter of former Arkansas Governor O.A. Hadley, who owned a nearby 4,000-acre ranch called The Clyde.

She is best known as the author of the 1959 classic about the Manhattan Project, The House at Otowi Bridge: The Story of Edith Warner and Los Alamos. As a poet and a social commentator through her writings, she had the distinction of being the only native New Mexican to participate in the modernist poetry movement that flourished in Santa Fe from the 1920s through the 1930s.

Peggy lived in Los Alamos for most of her life, where her father ran the Los Alamos Ranch School. At home for the summer after her first year at Smith College, she met Fermor Spencer Church, a young teacher at her father's school. They were married the following summer of 1924 and raised three sons.

Installation Site
In the town center of Los Alamos –
at Ashley Pond

· Luna County ·

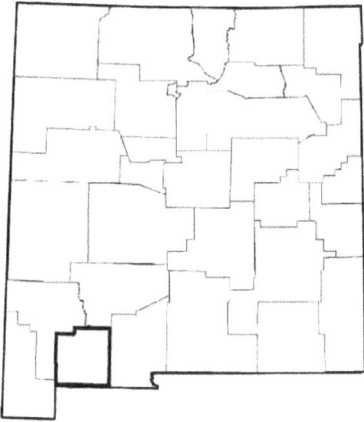

Luna County was named for Don Solomon Luna, a prominent political figure during the territorial days of New Mexico. It was created on March 16, 1901.

County Seat: Deming

Communities: Gage, Columbus and Hermanas

2,957 Square Miles

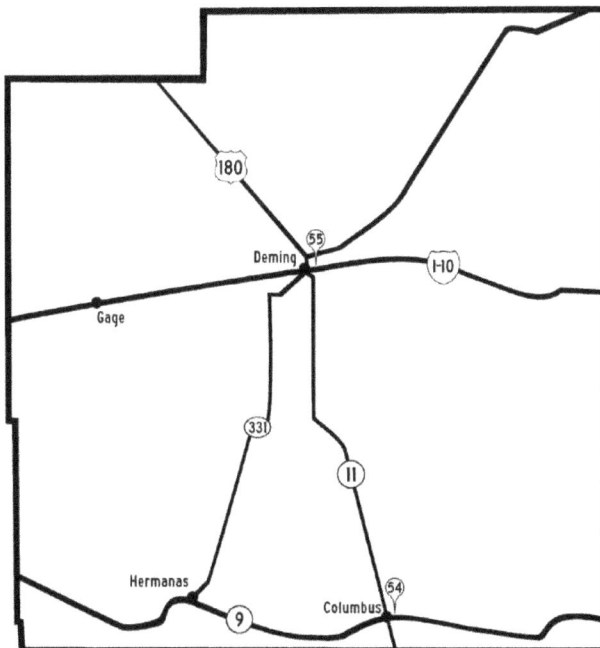

FIRST AERO SQUADRON AIRFIELD

The 1st Aero Squadron is the U.S. military's oldest aviation unit, created on March 5, 1913. In 1916 the squadron, which comprised 8 airplanes, 11 pilots, and 34 enlisted men, became the first U.S. Army air combat unit. As a response to Mexican revolutionary Francisco "Pancho" Villa's attack on Columbus, New Mexico, General John J. Pershing ordered the squadron to fly reconnaissance sorties from Columbus airfield on March 15, 1916.

The squadron, flying Curtiss JN-3s, known as Jennys, flew 540 sorties from March 1916 to January 1917. Jennys were used for aerial reconnaissance and photography and for delivering mail and official dispatch from airfields in Columbus and Casas Grandes, Mexico. Presently designated as the 1st Reconnaissance Squadron, the squadron is the oldest continuously active unit in the U.S. Air Force. Extant buildings dating from Villa's raid and Pershing's military response are located in nearby Pancho Villa State Park and the Village of Columbus and Camp Furlong National Historic Landmark district.

The 91st Aero Squadron was a unit of the Air Service of the United States Army that fought on the Western Front during World War I. The 91st was among the first five flying squadrons to arrive in France from the United States, arriving at Chaumont Hill on November 15, 1917.

Installation Site

On Highway 9 (Anapra Rd) at Kansas Street on the south side of the highway

MARY ANN DEMING CROCKER
(1827 – 1889)

Born in 1827, Mary Ann Deming was married to Charles Crocker, one of the founders of the Central Pacific Railroad. A "silver spike" was driven here in 1881 that commemorated connecting the Southern Pacific and Santa Fe railroads, and signaled completion of the nation's second transcontinental railroad. The new settlement was christened Deming in Mary's honor for her generosity and benevolence to many charitable causes for the poor.

Mary Ann's father, John Jay Deming's sawmill operations in Illinois made him a very wealthy man. She attended a private seminary school for girls in New York. She married Charles Crocker in 1852 and moved with him to California. He created a very successful general store in San Francisco, and he and Mary Ann became prominent citizens. He went on to establish the Central Pacific Railroad. They had four children who lived to adulthood – Charles Frederick Crocker, George Crocker, Harriet "Hattie" Valentine Alexander, and William Henry Crocker. It is unknown if Mary Ann ever visited Deming during her lifetime.

Installation Site
At the Deming Visitor Center - Near the train and welcome signal

· **McKinley County** ·

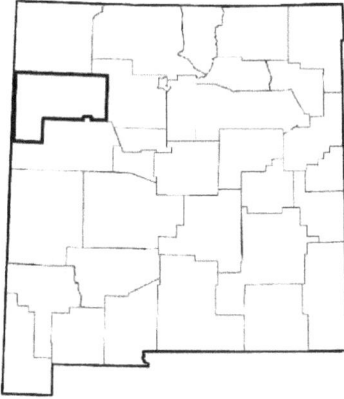

McKinley County was named after the twenty-fifth President, William McKinley. It was created February 23, 1899.

County Seat: Gallup

Communities: Churchrock, Thoreau, Zuni, White Horse, McGaffey and Crownpoint

5,461 Square Miles

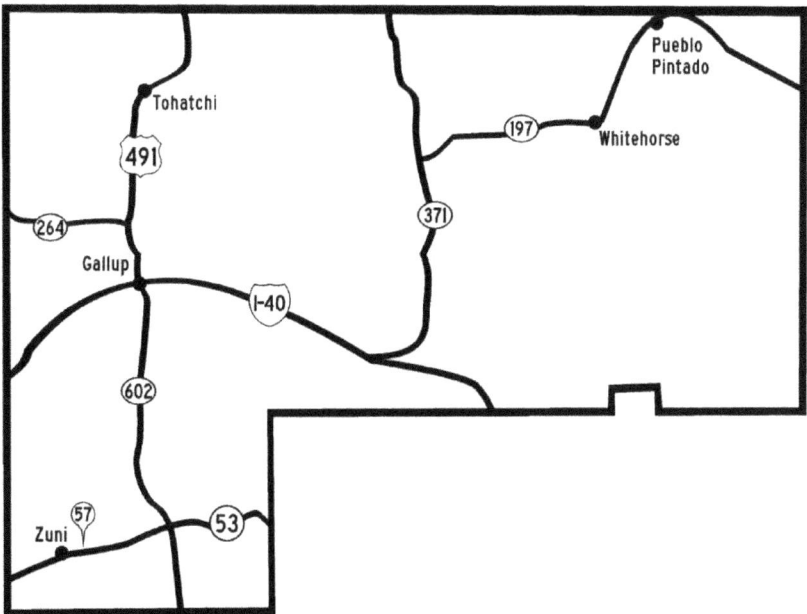

OLLA MAIDENS
ZUNI PUEBLO

The Zuni Olla Maidens are an all women's group known for their amazing skill and ability to balance fragile water jars or "ollas" on their heads.

Throughout history, Zuni women collected water in ollas from nearby springs on a daily basis. Today, these women perform in parades and community events. They are seen walking with water jars placed on their heads while singing their own compositions and those traditionally sung by Zuni men.

Zuni Olla Maidens are a group of Zuni Pueblo women traveling throughout North America, sharing their history and culture. They have become quite well known for using their skill and talent to dance to a drummer's beat while carrying water in clay water jars on their heads. For hundreds of years, the Zuni Olla Maidens have been transporting water from the surrounding springs for the people in their community.

The Zuni women have performed in numerous festivals and other events, including the Festival of American Folk Life and the Museum of Women in the Arts, both in Washington, D.C. They have also made presentations at smaller community events throughout Canada and the United States.

Further keeping their culture alive, the documentary film "Singing their Songs," includes the story of these women. This film is shown on college campuses throughout the United States.

<u>Installation Site</u>

In Zuni Pueblo on Route 301 at Pueblo Road - at Mile Marker 17

· Mora County ·

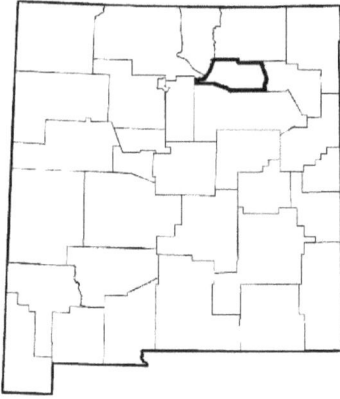

Mora County has the only unincorporated county seat in the state. Early documents refer to "Demora," meaning a camp or stopover, and it is still a beautiful place to rest.

County Seat: Mora

Communities: Watrous, Loma Parda, Wagon Mound, Cañoncito, Las Tusas, Buena Vista, Manuelitas, Guadalupita, and Golondrinas

5,461 Square Miles

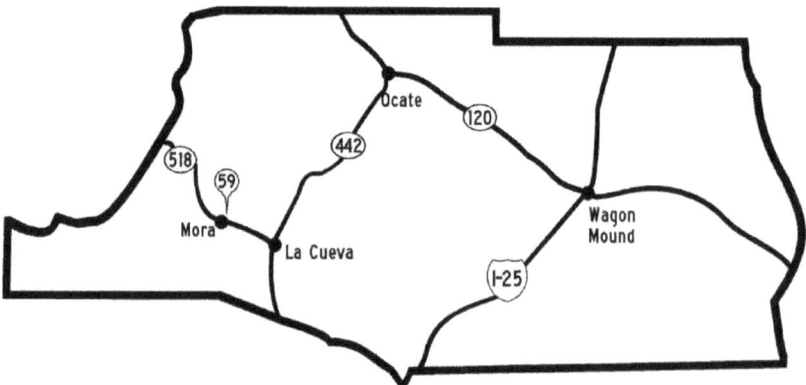

ST. VRAIN MILL
CERAN ST. VRAIN

The St. Vrain Mill is a stone, water-powered, vertical gristmill. The mill (molino de piedra in Spanish) was one of several in the Mora Valley that suppled flour and meal to nearby Fort Union in the mid-1800s. The mill was built in 1864 by Ceran St. Vrain after his wood mill in Taos burned. St. Vrain operated the mill until his death in 1870. The mill continued to supply flour and grain to Mora Valley residents until 1933. After years of neglect, rehabilitation of the began in 2015.

Ceran de Hault de Lassus de St. Vrain was born in 1802 in French territory near St. Louis, Missouri. At the age of 16, he worked as a clerk and fur trader for the Bernard Pratte and Company. In 1824 he made his first of many trading trips on the Santa Fe Trail. By the 1830s St. Vrain partnered with Charles Bent in a trading enterprise operating in Wyoming, Kansas, Colorado and northern New Mexico. During the 1850s St. Vrain concentrated his businesses in the Mora Valley, operating several sawmills and Mora's first gristmill. At the time of his death in 1870, he was one of the most prominent men in northern New Mexico.

The St. Vrain Mill was added to the National Register of Historic Places in 1972. In 2002, it was placed on the list of the ten most historical places in New Mexico. Then in 2013, the Saint Vrain Mill Preservation and Historical Foundation Inc. were established, and the foundation signed a purchase agreement with the owner in 2014.

The rehabilitation of the Mill has been ongoing. The eventual end-use of the Mill will be a Mora Valley Heritage Center, showcasing the history of the generational families of the county.

Installation Site

Highway 434, Mile Marker 13 - In the parking lot of the St. Vrain Mill Foundation

· Otero County ·

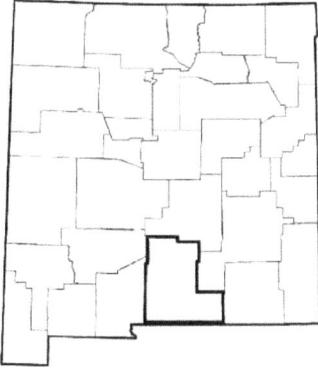

Otero County was created in 1899 and named for Miguel Otero, the Territorial Governor of New Mexico at the time.

County Seat: Alamogordo

Communities: Oro Grande, Piñon, Mayhill, Sunspot, Cloudcroft, Three Rivers, Tularosa, Mountain Park, Mescalero and Bent

6,638 Square Miles

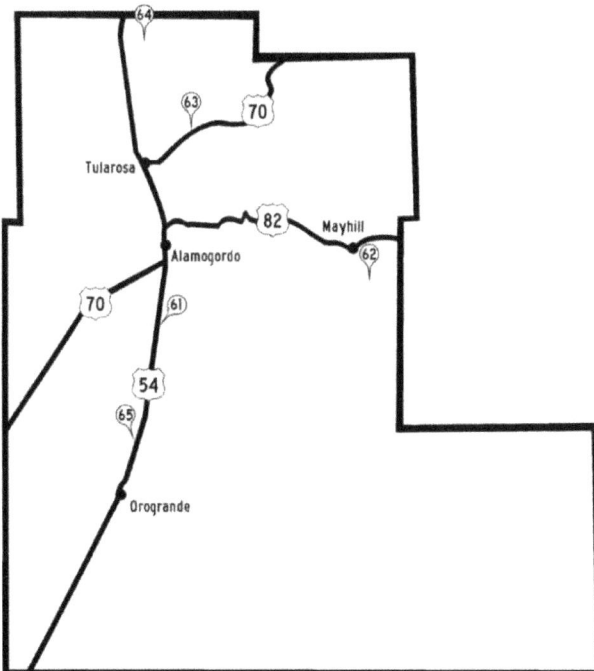

THREE RIVERS PETROGLYPH SITE

Three miles east of here is one of the most concentrated arrays of petroglyphs in the Southwest. Along a mile-long volcanic ridge are some 21,000 images depicting animals, humans, plants and geometric shapes making it one of very few sites with public access to so many examples of rock art. The glyphs were etched into dense basalt rock with stone tools by the Jornada Mogollon people ca. 900-1400 A.D. Sierra Blanca Peak towers above site.

These petroglyphs are located midway between Tularosa and Carrizozo in Otero County on Highway 54. These outstanding examples of prehistoric rock art can be easily viewed from a trail open to the public.

<u>Installation Site</u>
US 54, Mile Marker 97
at the new pull-out on highway widening

JOHN PRATHER
(1875 – 1965)
"MULE KING"

Rancher John Prather worked well with the federal government through two world wars. From his 32,000-acre ranch atop Otero Mesa, he ran New Mexico's largest Army mule-breeding program. But in 1957, the government condemned his land for part of McGregor Missile Range. Prather rebuffed the military and remained on his ranch. His story made national headlines and is told in the book and movie "Fire on the Mountain."

At 82, John Prather was given a court order evicting him from his land by three U. S. Marshals. The Army needed Prather's and his neighbor's ranches to test the next generation of warfare devices as part of the McGregor Missile Range. After a three-hour standoff, with the Marshals blocking Prather's way to his house and with Prather armed only with a hoof-knife, the Marshals gave up. After Prather died in 1965 at the age of 90, the McGregor Missile Range bought his land. However, Prather was buried next to his wife on the property.

Installation Site
US 54 between Mile Markers 42 and 46

"MISS MAC" PIONEER WOMAN
(1870 – 1956)

After disembarking from the RMS Lucania at Ellis Island in 1902, Jessie MacMillan bought her first six-shooter in New York before traveling alone to the Sacramento Mountains to settle her homestead, patented in 1908. A privileged life at European boarding schools did not deter her from hard work. She introduced the first alfalfa crop in the area and rode many miles on her horse, Wee Boy, to tutor the local ranch children. Her saddle is on display at the Sacramento Historical Museum in Cloudcroft.

Jessie MacMillan was born in England in 1870 into a wealthy family. After her father's death, her inheritance would mean she would not have to work or be concerned about money for the rest of her life. Instead, she chose a different type of life in America.

When Congress amended the Homestead Act in 1867 to include single women, at 30, Jessie decided to move to New Mexico and take advantage of the opportunity. She turned away from her life of privilege there to secure a homestead in the Sacramento Mountains. Much has yet to be written about the life she led at her homestead.

Installation Site
NM 24 at Mile Marker 8.3 on the south side

ROUND MOUNTAIN

This cone-shaped mountain is a landmark in southern New Mexico that has historic significance for many area families. In April 1868 a skirmish occurred between the Apache and Tularosa settlers when six U.S. soldiers left supply wagons between Fort Stanton and Fort Seldon. The besieged travelers took refuge on Round Mountain. Each spring a fiesta is held in Tularosa to commemorate this battle.

Round mountain is located in Otero County in southern New Mexico, about 9 miles northeast of the town of Tularosa. It's located just off US Highway 70. The cone-shaped mountain has an elevation of 5977 feet. St. Francis de Paula Catholic Church was erected to fulfill a promise made by the people living in Tularosa that if they survived the battle, they would show their gratitude by building this church.

Installation Site
US 70 at Mile Marker 339.87 - North side of the highway – West of the bridge

TURQUOISE

Turquoise was founded as a train stop by the El Paso and Northeastern Railroad in 1898. By 1899, it had a brick depot, section house, and telegraph station. Turquoise soon became the largest livestock shopping point in Otero County. Cattle and sheep holding pens were built with capacities of over 1,000 animals, which filled hundreds of stock cars. The livestock was transported to markets around the country. International Sheep Company warehoused and the Orogrande Water Company headquarters were located there.

By the turn of the 20th century, there were 15 buildings in the community, including a restaurant. In 1910, 6,000 cattle and sheep were shipped from the station. During World War I and World War II, horses and mules were shipped from the station to fulfill U.S. government contracts. By the mid-1920s, Turquoise was a crossroads for automobile traffic on highways 3 and 366. The area was abandoned in the late 1950s to early 1960s.

Charles Eddy founded the El Paso and Northeastern Railway, a short line railroad built at the beginning of the twentieth century. It was built to connect the El Paso, Texas, industrial center with the United States National Transportation hub in Chicago. He also was instrumental in establishing the now abandoned town of Turquoise, which was thriving in the mid-1920s.

<u>Installation Site</u>

NM 506, Mile Marker 40.62
at the intersection with US 54

· Quay County ·

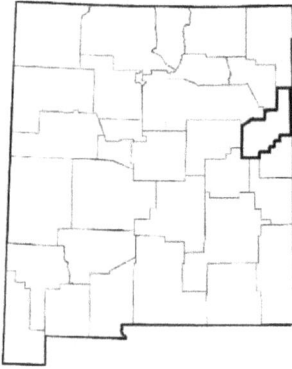

Quay County and its smallest settlement, Quay, were named for Matthew S. Quay, a U.S. Senator from Pennsylvania who helped spearhead the effort to turn the Territory of New Mexico into the State of New Mexico. It was created in 1903.

County Seat: Tucumcari

Communities: Logan, Nara Visa, San Jon, Forrest, McAlister, House, Rayland, Montoya and Glenrio

2,875 Square Miles

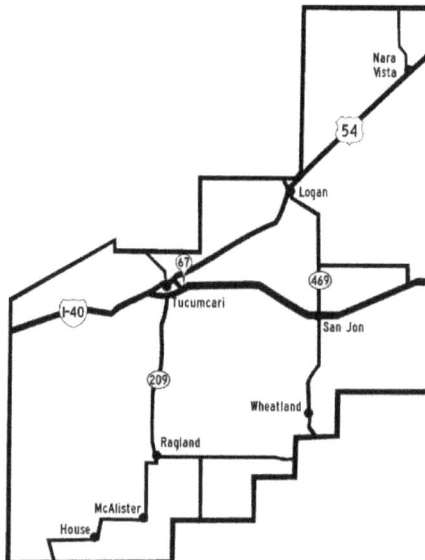

YETTA KOHN
(1843 – 1917)

Born is Bavaria and widowed in Las Vegas, New Mexico, Yetta ran the family store and raised four children alone. She later moved to La Cinta on the Canadian River where she opened another store, became the postmistress, started a bank and operated a ferry. She eventually bought land that eventually became the 4V Ranch, which expanded to the 4-T Cattle Company, operated today by her descendants.

Born is Bavaria and widowed in Las Vegas, New Mexico, Yetta ran the family store and raised four children alone. She later moved to La Cinta on the Canadian River where she opened another store, became the postmistress, started a bank and operated a ferry. She eventually bought land that eventually became the 4V Ranch, which expanded to the 4-T Cattle Company, operated today by her descendants.

Yetta Marie Goldsmith arrived in the United States in 1853, settling in Kansas. When she was 17, she married Samuel Kohn, a merchant. The couple has six children, although two died in their childhood. The couple moved their family several times in search of opportunity. In 1868, they decided to move to Las Vegas, New Mexico, where Samuel opened a store and Yetta worked as a seamstress.

When Yetta's husband died in 1878, at the age of 41, Yetta was just 35. She and her son Howard continued to run the thriving hide and wool shop.

She sold the shop at a profit and moved her family to La Cinta and opened a general store. She also bought land and cattle, became the town's postmistress, ran a ferry that crossed the Canadian River and was involved in many community activities. In 1890, Yetta and her family purchased the property in Montoya, New Mexico that became the T4 Cattle Ranch, her greatest legacy. She passed away in 1917 at the age of 74 and the ranch continued. The family has owned this successful ranch for six generations.

Installation Site
On Old Route 66 in the town of Tucumcari

· Rio Arriba County ·

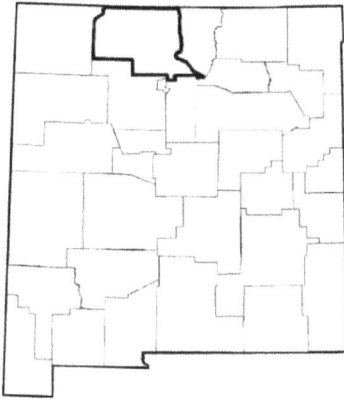

Rio Arriba, meaning "Upper River," was the Spanish designation for the upper Rio Grande River area. Created in 1852, the county was one of the seven original regions under Spanish rule.

County Seat: Tierra Amarilla

Communities: El Rito, Española, La Madera, Chama, Vallecitos, San Juan, Ojo Caliente, Tres Piedras, Abiquiu, and Los Ojos

5,861 Square Miles

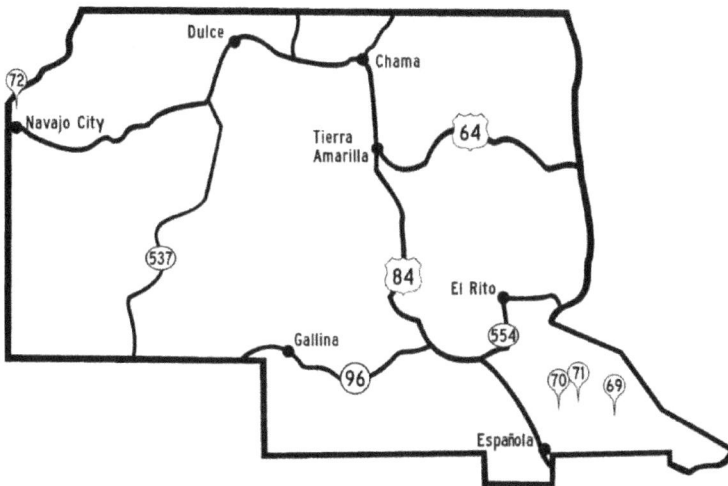

Córdova

Córdova, originally named Pueblo Quemado after a nearby burned-out Indian Pueblo, was permanently re-settled in 1750. It was renamed Córdova in 1900 after a prominent local family that had lived in the area since the Spanish Reconquest of 1692. The village chapel, San Antonio de Padue, is listed in the National Register of Historic Places and is an outstanding example of Northern New Mexico art and architecture. Córdova is home to a unique style of woodcarving begun by José Dolores López (1868-1937).

The town is between Santa Fe and Taos and was the home of the famous carver José Dolores López, known affectionately as "Dolores." López grew up in the fervent Catholicism of the region and, as a boy, watched his father, José Dolores López, carving Santos (Saints). He was a skilled carpenter and furniture maker who went on to create widely popular sculptures that were shown nationally.

Installation Site
NM 76 at Mile Marker 10.2

HISPANIC WOMEN OF COLONIAL NEW MEXICO AND THEIR WILL (1598 – 1821)
DOÑA MARGARITA MARTÍN

In Spanish Colonial New Mexico, women of all economic backgrounds had the legal right to draw up their own wills independent of their husbands.

Today, these are important historical documents and are a record of official estate inventories, land ownership, and relationships among extended family and heirs. Wills provide insights into women's socioeconomic status and illuminate the lives of women in Spanish Colonial New Mexico.

Margarita Martín was born in La Soledad sometime around 1700. She married twice, first to Juan Manuel Padilla in 1721 and then to Bernardo Roybal in 1731. Her will offers a view of items found in wealthy households during the Spanish Colonial era. Margarita owned a two-story house, land, orchards, household furnishings, religious items, and personal luxury items such as strings of pearls, slippers, shawls, linen, lace, and scarlet cloth. Notable among her possessions was a harp brought to New Mexico on an arduous journey over the Camino Real.

The settlement of her estate in Rio Arriba County is well documented in the New Mexico archives; however, they are written in Spanish.

Installation Site
Intersection of NM 68 and Los Luceros Road

LOS LUCEROS HACIENDA

Los Luceros was the headquarters of Sebastían Martín Serrano's 1703 land grant, which ran five miles along the Rio Grande and 128 miles east to the peaks of the Sangre de Cristo Mountains. Martín planted an extensive apple orchard that survives today on a former Tewa agricultural site. With Casa Grande – a rare two-story adobe with a double wraparound veranda – a chapel, jailhouse, Victorian cottage, and guesthouse, Los Luceros is one of a few surviving territorial haciendas in New Mexico. The Rio Arriba County Courthouse from 1846 to 1854, Wheelwright Museum founder Mary Cabot Wheelwright bought the dilapidated property in 1923 and remodeled it into a retreat for artists and writers of the period.

Herman Martin Serrano, a native of the Mexican mining town Zacatecas, was one of the soldiers who came with Juan de Oñate in 1508. He is the main forefather of the large Martin clan from which many New Mexicans have descended and is one of the few soldiers who decided to stay in the colony in 1601.

Installation Site
On US 68 between Mile Markers 8 and 9

98

NAVAJO LAKE STATE PARK
PINE RIVER

The U. S. Bureau of Reclamation built Navajo Dam between 1956 and 1962 as part of the Colorado River Storage Project. Navajo Lake State Park is the second largest in Ne Mexico. The Pine River recreational area has multiple campgrounds, one marina and boat ramp, and hiking trails. The visitors center was designed by the National Park Service in 1965 as part of its historically significant Mission 66 program. Early Native American Sites and ruins of the railroad towns Los Arboles and Rosa lie below the lake surface.

Navajo Lake is the second biggest lake in New Mexico, with several campgrounds, two marinas, and two boat docks. The lake has four developed recreational sites: San Juan River, Pine River, Sims Mesa in New Mexico, and Arboles in Colorado.

Installation Site
Highway 527 at Mile Marker 17 - Sims Mesa
Recreation Area

· Roosevelt County ·

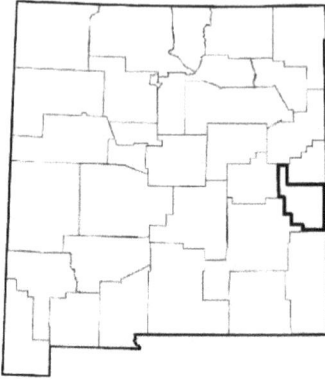

One of the five counties nationwide named for President Theodore Roosevelt, this county was created in 1903.

County Seat: Portales

Communities: Tolar, Floyd, Elida, Dora, Causey and Kenna

2,457 Square Miles

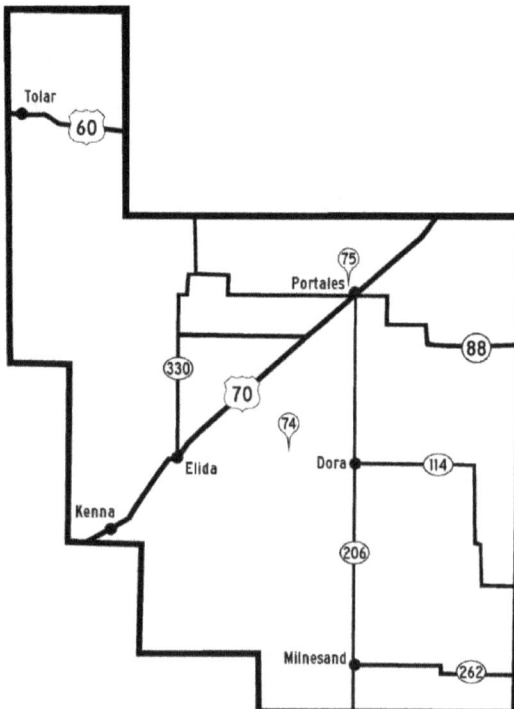

BUFFALO SOLDIER HILL

Near this spot in the summer of 1877, soldiers of Troop A of the U.S. Tenth Cavalry endured substantial hardship. During an attempt to force a band of Kwahada Comanche warriors back to their reservation in Oklahoma, the soldiers became lost, went 96 hours without water, and four died. Also known as the Forlorn Hope or Lost Troop Expedition, Troop A was composed of some 40 Buffalo Soldiers (African American cavalry) under the command of Captain Nicholas M. Nolan and accompanied by 22 bison hunters.

The term "Buffalo Soldier" refers to the African American men who served in the four all-black army regiments founded after the Civil War in 1866. The Comanche and Apache tribes called them "Buffalo Soldiers" due to the men's kinky and curly hair texture, similar to buffalos. The name has also been credited to the fierce soldiers' reputation, like the buffalo in battle. These soldiers served at 11 of the 16 forts located in New Mexico.

Installation Site
NM 114, near junction at South Roosevelt Road
located near Lingo, New Mexico

ROSE POWERS WHITE
(1894 – 1969)

Rose Powers White worked tirelessly to compile histories of early pioneers of southwestern New Mexico. She publicized numerous articles and was frequently asked to lecture to organizations and school groups. She served as President of the New Mexico Folklore Society in 1953, and with her husband in R.E. "Eddie" White donated land to Eastern New Mexico University and to the School for Exceptional Children.

Rosalie Pierce Powers was born in Las Vegas, New Mexico, in 1894 to Neville and Stephen Powers. She graduated from the Las Vegas Normal School and taught English, Spanish, and math at Vaughn and Santa Rosa schools. In 1923 she married R.E. "Eddie" White and relocated to Portales in Roosevelt County.

She became fascinated with the stories of the pioneers that settled in the area. She began interviewing people in the area and recording their memories. She continued to expand her research about the settlers and the cowboys, writing newspaper and magazine articles published throughout New Mexico. She also became a member of the New Mexico Folklore Society, assisting Dr. T.M. Pearce in research for his book, "New Mexico Place Names."

Rose has been honored for countless achievements, including her tireless dedication to preserving the history of the early days on the plains of Eastern New Mexico.

Installation Site

US 70 at Mile Marker 429 - Near the
Black Water Draw Museum

· San Juan County ·

Named for the river and the nearby San Juan Mountains, San Juan County was once the home of diverse ancient cultures including Chaco and Anasazi. This county was created in 1887.

County Seat: Aztec

Communities: Farmington, Bloomfield, Shiprock, Kirtland and La Plata

5,516 Square Miles

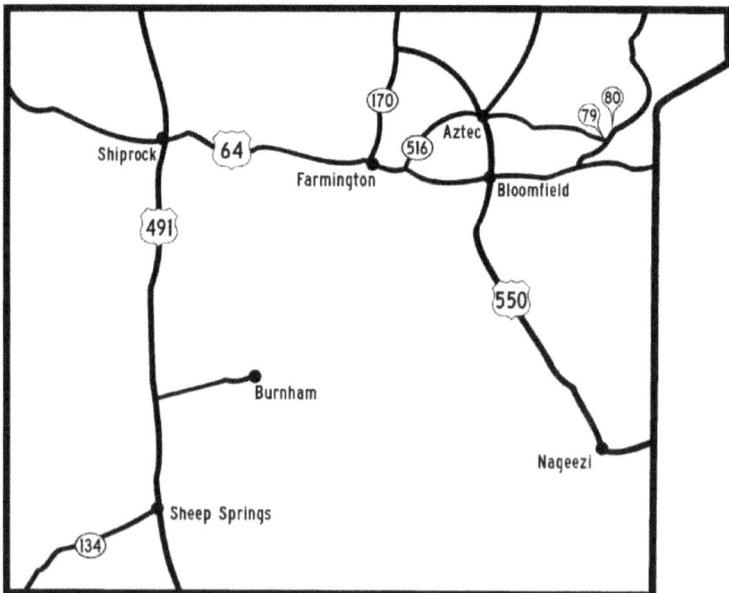

NAVAJO LAKE STATE PARK
SAN JUAN RIVER QUALITY WATER AREA

Cold, clear water released from Navajo Dam has created one of the best trout fishing areas in the Southwest. Special restrictions protect an area running 3.75 miles downstream from the dam, benefitting a valley with several wildlife habitats restored by the New Mexico Department of Game and Fish. The U.S. Bureau of Reclamation built Navajo Dam between 1956 and 1962 as part of the Colorado River Storage Project.

The San Juan River Quality Water Area consists of about 4.25 miles of the San Juan River located below Navajo Dam and Lake. It's among North America's most renowned trout fishing waters and is one of the top ten fly fishing destinations in the United States. The water released from the bottom of the dam is clear, cold, and rich in nutrients.

Installation Site
NM 511 at For Day-Use Area pull out

· San Miguel County ·

San Miguel was created by the territorial legislature of 1891, and derives its name from San Miguel del Vado, which translated is Saint Michael of the Ford. It is the area's largest community and was once a principal crossing for the Pecos River.

County Seat: Las Vegas

Communities: Montezuma, Sapello, Ledoux, Rociada, Pecos, Trujillo, Villanueva and Trementina

4,717 Square Miles

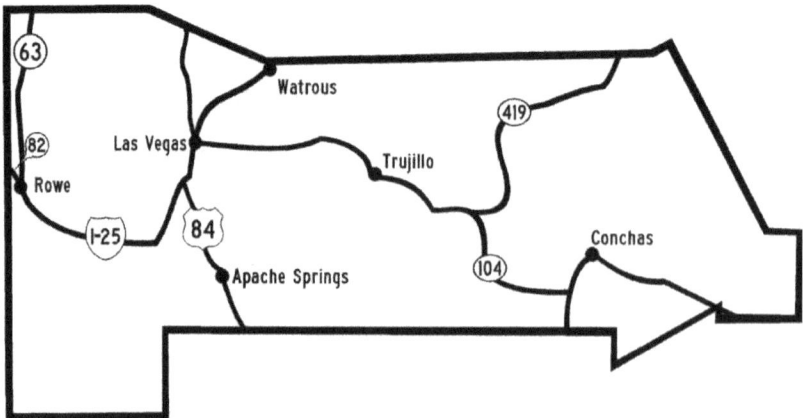

El VALLE COMMUNITY CENTER

Villaneuva, originally called La Cuesta, is one of the earliest Spanish colonial settlements along the Pecos River. The name was changed in 1890. In the 1940s, the Villanueva School was built, replacing a one-room schoolhouse. The school operated until the 1970s, when it was abandoned. Community efforts led to the revitalization of the building at the El Valle Community Center. The building houses the David F. Cargo Library, named for the former governor and used for community functions and educational activities.

El Valle includes many small communities, including the villages of San Juan and San Jose. The Pecos River runs through this valley, supplying water to the farms and fields through a system of acequias (irrigation canals) created over 200 years ago.

Installation Site
11 Los Pueblos Road, Villanueva

GLORIETA PASS BATTLEFIELD

The Civil War battle fought in this pass is often referred to as the "Gettysburg of the West." Union forces dashed the Confederacy's strategy to seize the Southwest's major supply base at Fort Union. Brigadier General Henry Hopkins Sibley's plan envisioned gaining control of the gold fields of Colorado, mineral-rich Nevada, the ports of California, as well as the northern Mexican states of Chihuahua, Sonora, and Baja California. Their defeat at the Battle of Glorieta Pass ended the Confederate's incursion into the Southwest.

The Texas vanguard captured Sana Fe, on March 10, 1862. On March 28 after two days of battle at the Glorieta Pass, Union troops, including Colorado and New Mexico volunteers, burned a poorly guarded Confederate supplies camp, spiked cannons, and slaughtered or freed hundreds of horses and mules. Within two weeks of their defeat here, Confederate troops were forced withdraw to Texas. This battlefield was designated a National Historic Landmark on November 5, 1961.

The Battle of Glorieta Pass was fought in the Sangre de Cristo Mountains in the northern New Mexico Territory from March 26-28, 1862. It became known as "Gettysburg of the West" because it was the most significant battle of the New Mexico Campaign during the Civil War. It destroyed the Confederate Army's goal of cutting off the West from the Union Army.

Installation Site

NM 63, one mile from I-25 Mile Marker 1

· Sandoval County ·

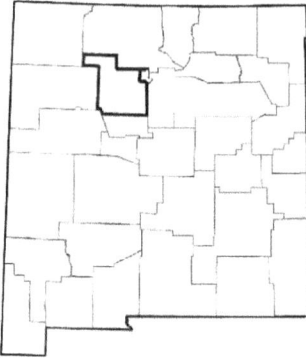

Sandoval County was created in 1903 and named for the Sandoval Family who lived in the area.

County Seat: Bernalillo

Communities: Corrales, Algadones, Cochiti Lake, Los Cerillos, La Bajada, Placitas and Peña Blanca

3,714 Square Miles

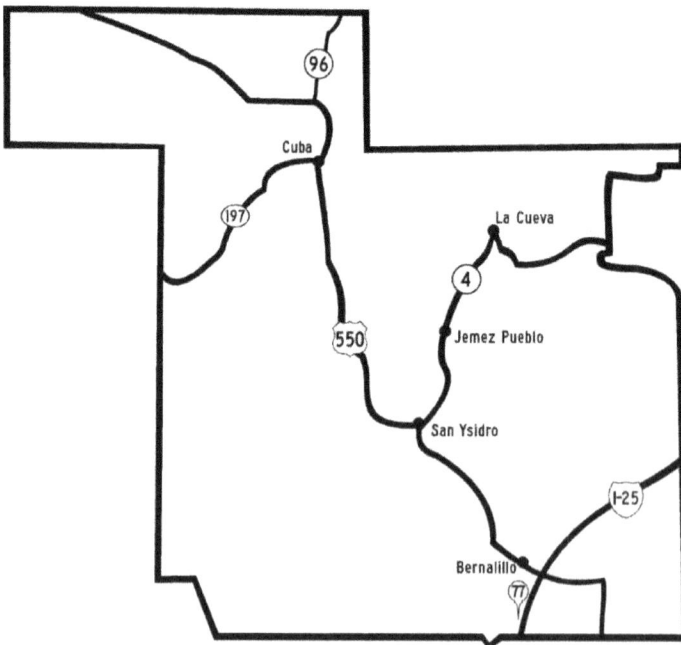

DULCELINA SALCE CURTIS
(1904 – 1995)

Teacher, agriculturalist, farmer and conservationist, Dulcelina Curtis led efforts to control flooding of arroyos in Corrales where a flood-control channel is named in her honor. The first woman appointed to a board of the U.S. Agricultural Stabilization and Conservation District, she received the National Endowment for Soil Conservation Award for New Mexico in 1988. She served on the Village Council and helped launch many of the town's civic organizations.

Dulcelina was a lifelong resident of Corrales. Her life's mission may have begun when, at just one-month-old, a flood washed her family's home away in 1904.

Then when she was only 14 years old, her mother died suddenly in the pandemic of 1918, leaving her the eldest of six siblings. Dulcelina met and married cowboy Vincent Curtis in 1928, having two daughters with him.

During the 1929 Depression, Corraleños were fortunate enough to grow their food because of the soil conservation efforts of people like Dulcelina. Passing away at the age of 91, she is recognized for her tireless effort to protect the community of Corrales from the flooding caused by the overflow of the arroyos, as well as other acts of leadership in the community.

Installation Site
NM 448 at Mile Marker 12

· Santa Fe County ·

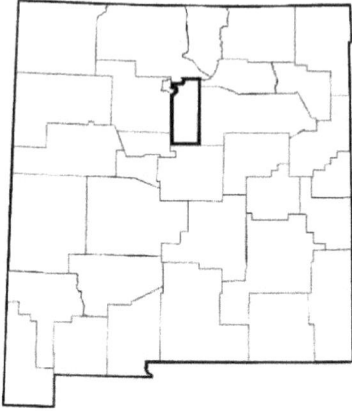

Santa Fe County was created in 1852 and was named for a city in Spain built by King Ferdinand and Queen Isabella. Santa Fe, New Mexico's capital, is the oldest capital in the United States.

County Seat: Santa Fe

Communities: Tesuque, Galisteo, Stanley, Madrid, Edgewood and Glorieta

4,717 Square Miles

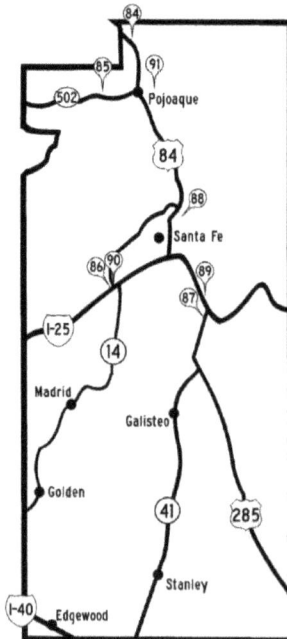

GALISTEO BASIN
SOUTHERN ROCKIES

The Galisteo Basin is a lowland of 730 square miles that has been continuously occupied since the Archaic period. It is bounded by the Sangre de Cristo Mountains on the north, Glorieta Mesa on the east, the San Pedro Mountains on the south, and La Bajada escarpment and the Rio Grande on the west. Due to its location between mountain ranges, the basin serves as an important transportation route between the Rio Grande Valley and Great Plains.

The foothills and higher peaks to the north are part of the Southern Rocky Mountains, which extend from southern Wyoming through Colorado and New Mexico. The Sangre de Cristo Mountains (Spanish for "Blood of Christ") trend from Salida, Colorado, in the north to Santa Fe in the south. The highest peak in New Mexico is Wheeler Peak northeast of Taos at 13,167 feet in elevation.

The Galisteo Basin lies right in the center of four ecoregions, including the southern Rocky Mountains, Southwestern Tablelands (includes parts of Colorado, New Mexico, Kansas, Texas, and Oklahoma), and mountains in Arizona and New Mexico. It is considered one of the most awe-inspiring archaeological sites in the United States.

Installation Site
US 285/84 South of Santa Fe near the
turnoff to Lamy

HISPANIC WOMEN OF COLONIAL NEW MEXICO AND MARRIAGE

DOÑA FRACISCA GÓMEZ ROBLEDO (1664 – 1766)

Marriages in Spanish Colonial New Mexico often served to forge alliances between powerful families. Women brought property, possessions, and money into marriages through dowries written into marriage contracts. Dowries were solely for the woman's future use and were used by her husband only with her permission. Many colonial women became matriarchs of family lines that continue in New Mexico today.

Francisca Gómez Robledo is representative of wealthy Spanish families in New Mexico in the 17th and 18th centuries. Born to a military family that descended from the Oñate expedition, she married Captain Ignacio Roybal in 1694. They had nine children and resided in a 17-room house in Jacona, where they managed sheep, cattle, oxen, horses, goats, and mules. Family possessions included military equipment and weapons, silver spoons and forks, and a bronze religious figure. Francisca died at age 102.

Francisca Gómez Robledo was born in San Ildefonso and died in Santa Fe at the remarkable age of 102. Records show that her mother, Ana, was killed during the Pueblo Revolt in 1680. The Robledo family ranch can be found near Santa Fe in the beautiful community of Jacona, New Mexico.

Installation Site

NM Highway 502 between Mile Marker 15 & 17

INEZ BUSHNER GILL
(1918 – 1982)
MARALYN BUDKE
(1936 – 2010)

Inez Bushner Gill impressed governors, legislators and journalists with her fiscal expertise. Among the original staff of the Legislative Council Service when it was founded in 1951, she served as fiscal analyst and principal staff for its finance committee. In 1957, she helped establish separate staff for what today is the Legislative Finance Committee. Inez developed many of the financial procedures that modernized state government and helped create the Department of Finance and Administration, bringing order to the chaos of state finances.

Maralyn Budke, Inez Gill's first intern, joined the Legislative Finance Committee in 1959 and was the first woman director from 1968-1982. A brilliant strategist and trusted advisor, Maralyn was a confidant to legislative leaders and chief of staff for Governors Cargo and Carruthers. Highly valued for her knowledge and insight, she mentored legislative and executive staff during 40 years of exemplary public service. Maralyn and Inez were two of the most important and influential women in New Mexico state government.

Inez Gill and Maralyn Budke made significant contributions to the New Mexico legislature. Inez impressed Governors, Legislators, and Journalists with her fiscal expertise. And Maralyn became Chief of Staff for New Mexico's Governor, David Cargo, just ten years after getting her undergraduate degree in political science from the University of New Mexico. That was just the beginning of Maralyn's extraordinary life.

Installation Site
In Santa Fe on the Capitol grounds

ROUTE 66

You are traveling an early alignment of U.S. 66, perhaps the most well-known road to follow this historic transportation corridor. A Spanish mission trail to Pecos Pueblo, the Santa Fe Trail and the National Old Trails Road all predate the Mother Road in using this narrow passage through rock terrain. Until the 1930s, Route 66 was aligned through downtown Santa Fe, exited the city to the southwest, traversed La Bajada and passed through the famed "Big Cut" before descending into Albuquerque. In 1937, Santa Fe was bypassed and Route 66 straightened, creating a direct east-west alignment that eliminated 197 miles of travel.

Route 66 was completed in 1926, taking travelers east to west from Chicago to Los Angeles. Although the route was changed and upgraded in 1937, there are nearly 400 miles of Route 66 located in the State of New Mexico. Thousands of travelers have taken this fascinating road trip through New Mexico.

Installation Site
On NM 300 at Mile Marker 6

VIRGINIA GUTIERREZ
(1941 – 2011)

Accomplished potter and Nambe Pueblo's first woman lieutenant governor, Virginia's work has appeared in the Smithsonian Museum and in galleries around the world. As a young girl, she learned her trade from a great aunt and became particularly well known for her distinctive plates. She helped support her family by selling her work, although she gave much of it away to family and friends. A proud member of her Pueblo, she spoke Tewa fluently and served honorably as lieutenant governor in 1991 and 1992.

Virginia Gutierrez is a well-known potter from the Pojoaque Pueblo. While experimenting with colors, she produced polychrome plates and jars. She used micaceous clay, creating exciting colors from smoke and fire. Her contributions as an artist and leader of the Nambe Pueblo are remarkable.

Installation Site
On NM State Road 503 in Nambe

HISPANIC WOMEN OF COLONIAL NEW MEXICO AND THE LAW

DOÑA ANTONIA MORAGA
(1649 – 1749)

During the Colonial period in New Mexico, Spanish law granted women important legal rights. Women conducted land deals, purchased property and livestock, operated businesses, kept their surnames, and wrote will independent of their husbands. Women offered testimony in legal cases and addressed legal matters in court. Inheritance laws provided that a daughter receive a portion of the estate equal to her male siblings.

Antonia Moraga, who lived in the Chimayo valley during the 17th and 18th centuries, raised ten children and managed the family's farm operation. The Spanish Colonial family herded sheep, hunted buffalo, and wove cloth. Her husband, Cristóbal Martín Serrano, was blind. In his stead, Antonia managed the family's property and appeared in court several times from 1695 to 1716 to testify on boundary disputes and land ownership. In 1713 she filed a lawsuit to secure ownership of land as part of her grandfather's estate.

Living to 80 years old, Doña Antonia Moraga's long life included managing an extensive farming operation and dealing with countless legal issues when most women didn't handle such responsibilities. She was an impressive role model for women.

Installation Site

In Santa Cruz at the intersection of Calle de la Cañada and NM 76

HISPANIC WOMEN OF COLONIAL NEW MEXICO AND THE LAW

Doña Rosa Bustamante
(1735 – 1814)

During the colonial period in New Mexico, Spanish law granted women important legal rights. Women conducted land deals, purchased property and livestock, operated businesses, kept their surnames, and wrote wills independent of their husbands. Women offered testimony in legal cases and addressed legal matters in court. Inheritance laws provided that a daughter receive a portion of the estate equal to her male siblings.

Rosa Bustamante (1735-1814) was a successful businesswoman in northern New Mexico in the 18th and 19th centuries. Born to wealthy descendants of the Oñate expedition, she owned a weaving store in Santa Fe and married Antonio José Ortiz, the city's alcalde. Her large dowry was valued at 2,179 pesos. Rosa owned a mill, sheep cattle, orchards, and property in Pojoaque, Santa Fe, and La Ciénega. She was generous to her community, served as godmother to 64 children, and became the largest benefactor of the Catholic Church for that time.

Rosa is the daughter of Bernardo Bustamonte Y Tagle and Feliciana Vega y Coco, wealthy descendants of Oñate expedition. She and her husband, Antonia José Ortiz, spent an active life growing their family to include ten children, expanding their business interests to ranches across the state, and establishing trade between Santa Fe and Mexico.

Installation Site
I-25 West Frontage Road - In La Cienega and Entrada la Cienega

HISPANIC WOMEN OF COLONIAL NEW MEXICO AND LAND OWNERSHIP

VEGA Y COCA SISTERS
FELICIANA, LEONARDA, MARÍA, FRANCISCA AND ISABEL

Under Spanish law, women in New Mexico could buy, sell, and own property. A woman did not need her husband's permission to sell property that she brought into the marriage, and further, she could use the court system to adjudicate land claims. Several communities in New Mexico, such as La Cíenega and Pajarito, arose on combined lad grants owned in part or whole by women.

The Vega y Coca sisters were born between 1700 and 1712 to Miguel Vega y Coca, a soldier and alcalde in Taos, Santa Cruz, and Santa Fe. His wife was Ignacia Montoya. In 1730 the family moved to La Cíenega where Miguel died in 1751. Each daughter inherited property, including an extensive plot of land, a large house, and pasturelands. The sisters married soldiers, alcaldes, and landowners, leaving a legacy of prominent Spanish families in New Mexico. Among their descendants are members of the Alire, Baca, Bustamante, Ortiz, and Tenorio families.

The sons Diego Manuel and Cristôbal married two sisters, María and Polonia de la Vega y Coca of Santa Fe, on the same day. Daughter Feliciana of Miguel de la Vega y Coca married Don Bernardo de Bustamante, and all of these families left their descendants in New Mexico.

Installation Site

I-25 West Frontage Road in La Cienega and
Entrada La Cienega

· Sierra County ·

Sierra County was named for the Sierra De los Caballos range of mountains. It was created in April 1884. The dry climate, cool lakes, and hot mineral springs draw thousands of visitors annually.

County Seat: Truth or Consequences

Communities: Hillsborough, Kingston, Caballo, Elephant Butte, Monticello and Winston

4,231 Square Miles

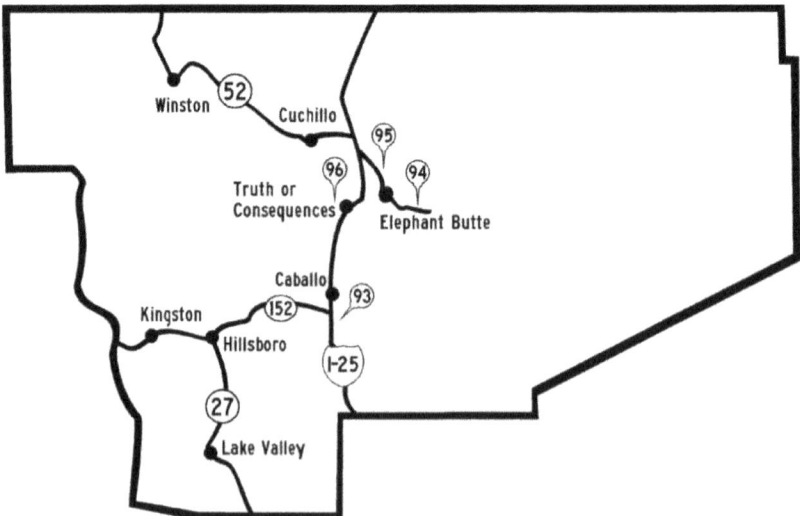

CABALLO MOUNTAINS

The rugged Caballo Mountains are notable for their complex geologic history revealed in a variety of surface rocks. The lowest slopes are composed of ancient granites from the Proterozoic Eon more than two billion years ago while sedimentary sandstones, limestones, and dolomites date to the subsequent Paleozoic Era when this area was a shallow tropical sea.

Tectonic activity uplifted the Caballos through the earth's crust at the edge of the Rio Grande Rift. Said to resemble the head of a horse, they sometimes are identified as the Sierra Caballo on maps.

The Caballo Mountains are in both the Sierra and Doña Ana Counties in New Mexico. The word "Caballo" means "horse" in Spanish. The mountains are east of the Rio Grande and Caballo Lake and west of Jornada del Muerto. The south end of the range extends into northwest Doña Ana County.

Installation Site
NM Highway 187 on Mile Marker 24.3

ELEPHANT BUTTE DAM

Pueblo Indians irrigated and farmed the Rio Grande Valley for centuries before the Spaniards arrived and built acequias. Building the dam was the first large-scale effort to harness and control the Rio Grande. Its construction proved critical to the historic debate over interstate and international water use. Built between 1910-1916, Elephant Butte Dam when completed was the world's second largest irrigation reservoir with a capacity of more than two million acre-feet of water. It revolutionized agricultural production in southern New Mexico. The dam irrigates 178,000 acres of land, aids in flood control, produces hydroelectric power, and created a park with boating, fishing, hiking, and camping facilities.

Elephant Butte Reservoir is a reservoir located five miles north of Truth or Consequences in New Mexico on the Rio Grande River. It is the largest reservoir in New Mexico and the 84th largest in the United States, and the town of Elephant Butte is known as the "Diamond in the Desert."

Installation Site
NM Highway 51 at Mile Marker 4.1

JORNADA DEL MUERTO

This section of the Camino Real is called the Jornada del Muerto or Deadman's Journey after the tragic fate of German trader Bernardo Gruber, El Alemán. In 1670 the Inquisition accused him of witchcraft. He escaped and attempted to cross ninety miles of forbidding desert south of Socorro, between the Paraje de Fray Cristóbal to the north and the Paraje de Robledo to the south.

After days of unquenched thirst, Gruber's Apache servant Antonio went in search of water. When he returned, El Alemán was gone. Weeks later, travelers found his clothing and his scattered remains. Spanish and Mexican merchants, the U.S. Army, the Texas Confederates in 1862, and the railroad in 1880s also used this route.

The Jornada del Muerto runs about 100 miles from north to south, remaining almost entirely uninhabited and undeveloped to the present day.

Installation Site
NM Highway 51 at Mile Marker 15

MAGNIFICENT MAGNOLIA
(1893 - 1974)

Magnolia Ellis was a "magnetic healer." Born in Hill County, Texas, she settled in Hot Springs, today's Truth or Consequences, in 1937, and built a two-story residence and office that is listed in the National Register of Historic Places. She denied being a faith healer, instead laying hands on patients who claimed to have a feeling of electricity when she touched them. Patients picked numbers, and Magnolia visited them in six different booths, sometimes seeing 100 patients a day. Magnificent Magnolia helped put Hot Springs on the map.

Magnolia has been acknowledged by doctors nationally because of her healing gifts. In addition, New Mexico governors have recognized her because of her contributions to the state, making her a tremendous role model for women.

Installation Site
In Truth or Consequences at the intersection of Main and Broadway_between E. Riverside Dr.
and S. Riverside Drive

· Socorro County ·

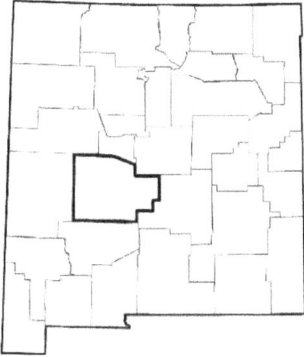

Socorro County was created in 1852 and was the first county in New Mexico. It was named for the local pueblo.

County Seat: Socorro

Communities: Abeytas, Alamillo, Alamo, Magdalena, San Antonio, San Antonito and LaJoya

4,231 Square Miles

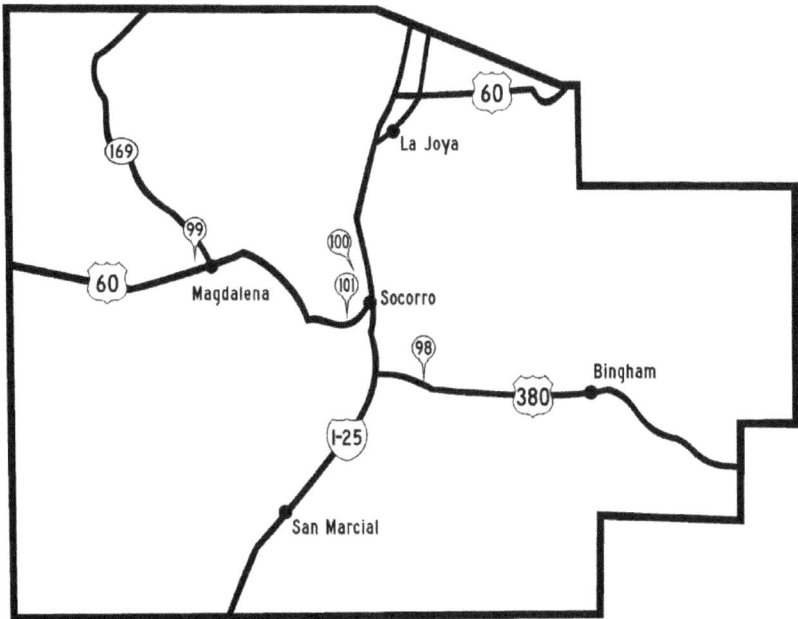

CARTHAGE – TOKAY – FRALEY

In the 1860s soldiers exploited a coal field east of San Antonio for heating fuel and for their smithies. Mining activity surged after 1883 when the Santa Fe railroad laid track to the Carthage coal field. Carthage was the site of the first sustained coal mining in New Mexico and had periods of significant activity until the 1960s, producing more than two million tons of coal. Tokay, southwest of Carthage, was founded in 1915. Coal production there steadily increased until the late 1920s when it began to decline. By the 1940s mining had ceased. Fraley, a town that developed around kilns processing high-quality lime, died when the rail line was removed in 1900.

Although the towns of Carthage, Tokay, and Fraley are little more than ghost towns today, they were thriving coal mining towns in the early 1900s due to the railroad that once ran from San Antonio to Carthage. The section on the line known as the San Pedro (Carthage) Branch was an essential short-line operation for the Santa Fe Railroad.

August H. "Gus" Hilton owned one of those early mines. He established himself as the leading merchant and trader in San Antonio, New Mexico, and became the head of one of the wealthiest families in the United States today.

Installation Site
US 380 at Mile Marker 9.4

KELLY

Silver was discovered in Kelly around 1866 and the town site was laid out in circa 1879. Kelly boomed with silver mining and eventually zinc mining, becoming one of central New Mexico's most prosperous mining towns. At one time, it boasted a population of 3,000. When zinc played out in the 1930s, Kelly began to die and is now a ghost town.

Kelly prospered in the 1880s after lead and silver discoveries around 1866. But it was the discarded zinc carbonate – vital in paint manufacturing – that made Kelly boom in the early 1900s. Stores, banks, saloons, schools, and churches lined its streets and the population reached 3,000. When the mines played out in the 1930s, Kelly became a ghost town, its homes hauled to Magdelena. A preserved church stands near ruined mine works, and the Kelly Mine head shaft – a 121-foot-high structure built from a design by Alexander G. Eiffel for Carnegie Steel Works – still towers over the site.

By 1884, Kelly Township had banks, churches, saloons, a clinic, and mercantile stores. It was named after Patrick H. Kelley, who held a number of the mining claims. The nearby village of Magdalena, New Mexico, three miles north of Kelly, was the home of the AT & SF Railway terminal established to haul away the precious ores from these mines.

The last residents of Kelly left the town in 1947, moving most of their homes to Magdalena. Although Kelly became a ghost town, Magdalena remains a ranching community.

Installation Site
US 60 at Mile Marker 112.8

NEW MEXICO TECH

The New Mexico Institute of Mining and Technology is consistently ranked as one of the top research universities in science and technology. Originally established as the New Mexico School of Mines, it was one of the original colleges established by the territorial legislature in 1889, with Agriculture and Mechanic Arts, now New Mexico State University, in Las Cruces. The school specializes in science and engineering, offering doctorate-level degrees, and conducts extensive research and development. It is headquarters for the Very Large Array located 60 miles west of here.

Although New Mexico Tech is a relatively small university with approximately 1500 students enrolled each year, it is known internationally for the strength of its academic programs and focus on research.

Installation Site
On the intersection of College and
Leroy Avenues in Socorro

SOCORRO

Socorro derives its name from Juan de Oñate, whose caravan in 1598 had traversed the Jornada del Muerto of El Camino Real and was provided maize by the Piro Indian pueblo Teypama on the Rio Grande's west bank. Oñate rechristened the village using the Spanish word for succor, socorro. The name was later transferred to the nearby pueblo Pilabó, the site of present-day Socorro, where the Spanish built Nuestra Señora de Perpetuo Socorro in 1626. Abandoned in the 1680 Pueblo Revolt, the area was resettled in 1815 and the mission rebuilt as San Miguel Church in 1821. It was listed in the National Register of Historic Places in 2016.

The city of Socorro is the county seat of Socorro County, located in New Mexico's Rio Grande Valley, 74 miles south of Albuquerque and 146 miles north of Las Cruces., with an elevation of 4,579 feet. It serves the surrounding ranching and farming communities. In 2020 the population was 8,900.

Installation Site
US 60 at Mile Marker 137-138 and at City Hall,
111 School of Mines Road

· Taos County ·

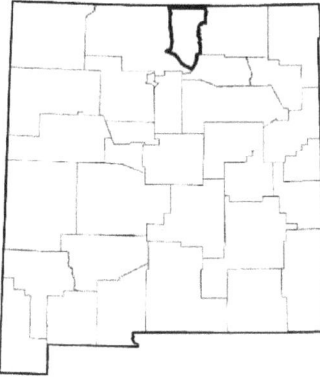

In 1852 Spanish explorers discovered an inhabited pueblo in the area for which Taos County and its seat were named.

County Seat: Taos

Communities: Questa, Arroyo Seco, Talpa and Ranchos de Taos

2,257 Square Miles

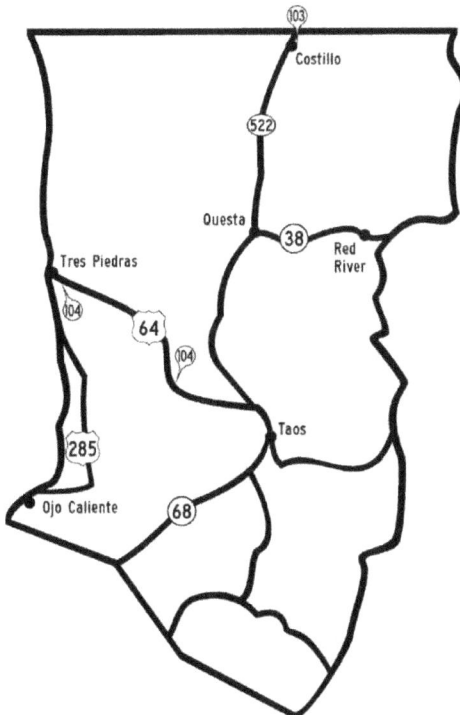

MARIA JOSEFA JARAMILLO CARSON
(1828-1868)

A descendant of Spanish settlers, Josefa Jaramillo was born in Potrero in 1828 to a prominent family. She was baptized in the Santa Cruz de la Cañada Church in Santa Cruz. In 1843 she married Christopher "Kit" Carson, the famous frontiersman, expedition leader and Army officer. Carson was often away for years at a time, leaving Josefa to manage the large family home in Taos.

During the 1847 Taos Rebellion, while Kit Carson was away, Josefa escaped an attack at her brother-in-law Charles Bent's house by digging a hole through an adobe wall leading into an adjoining dwelling. Kit Carson retired from the U.S. Army in 1867, and the family moved to Boggsville, Colorado. Josefa died on April 23, 1869, a few days after the birth of her ninth child.

Josefa's father was a successful merchant, and her mother owned substantial acreage in the Rio Grande area of New Mexico. Kit Carson met and fell in love with Josef, a young, beautiful, and intelligent woman. He converted to Catholicism to obtain her father's blessing to marry her. They were married for 26 years. Josefa passed away at 40 years old, with Kit dying just months after her death.

Installation Site
US Highway 64/Kit Carson Road near the intersection
of Mariposa Place

RIO COSTILLA VALLEY

A winter hunting ground for many indigenous people, this area was originally homeland for the Ute people. In 1849, striving to encourage occupation on the Sangre de Cristo Land Grant, seven plazas were settled along the Rio Costilla. Governor Diego de Vargas crossed this valley during his reconquest of New Mexico to Spain from 1692-1697, as did Juan Bautista de Anza during his 1779 Comanche campaign.

The Rio Costilla Cooperative Livestock Association (RCCLA) has managed the Rio Costilla Valley since 1942. The area covers about 80,000 acres of wilderness, streams, lakes, and mountain ranges, including Ventero Peak, with elevations of over 12,000 feet.

Installation Site
NM Highway 522 in Costilla

RIO GRANDE GORGE BRIDGE

The Rio Grande Gorge and the Sangre de Cristo Mountains form a spectacular setting for the seventh highest bridge in the U.S. The deck sits 650 feet above the river. Completed in 1965 under the leadership of Gov. Jack M. Campbell, it established and east-west shipping and transportation corridor in northern New Mexico and is the only major bridge crossing the Rio Grande for over 100 miles. Spanning 1,272 feet, this elegantly designed deck truss bridge is in the National Register of Historic Places for its exceptional importance in transportation and engineering.

The Gorge Bridge is a steel deck arch bridge that spans across the Rio Grande Gorge 10 miles northwest of Taos, New Mexico. The bridge is the fifth highest bridge in the United States. There is also a popular walking trail along the rim of the gorge.

Installation Site
Two Markers, Two Locations
US 064/Intersection 285
US 522 at mile marker 2

· Torrance County ·

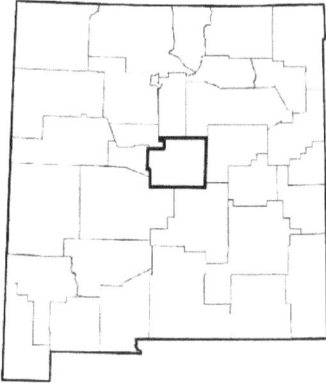

Torrance County was created in 1903 and named for Francis J. Torrance, a promoter who took part in building the New Mexico Central Railroad.

County Seat: Estancia

Communities: Mountainair, Tajique, Clines Corners, Encino, McIntosh, Manzano, Moriarty and Willard

3,355 Square Miles

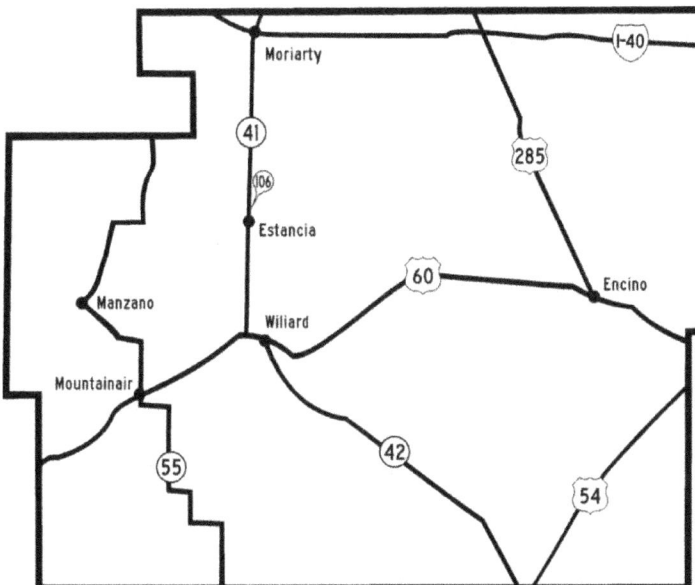

HOMESTEADER MARY ELLEN "MOLLIE" HALL WARREN KLAPP
(1862 – 1933)

Eighty-million acres of public land in the West went into private ownership by 1900 through the 1862 Homestead Act. New Mexico drew hundreds of settlers who built homes and farmed 160-acre allotments in pursuit of a better life. Mollie Klapp was one. Born in Illinois by 1900 she was widowed in Oklahoma with seven children when she decided to move to Moriarty, a "pinto bean capital of the world." The Estancia Valley is well-suited to dryland farming and helped New Mexico become the nation's fourth largest pinto bean producer by 1916 when 2.5 million pounds were harvested. Mollie farmed, taught school, and remarried. Her hard life led to institutionalization at the state mental health hospital in Las Vegas where she worked as a seamstress and housekeeper, and died from "exhaustion."

Mary Ellen "Mollie" Hall married Henry Walton Warren in Dade, Missouri relocating with him to the Cherokee Nation Territory in Oklahoma, giving birth to seven children. When Henry died in 1899, Mollie became a homesteader with her second husband, Andrew Klapp, in 1910, relocating to McIntosh, New Mexico. Andrew passed away in 1922, and she went on to live another eleven years, passing away in 1933 at 71 years old.

Installation Site

NM 41, near County Road A103

· Union County ·

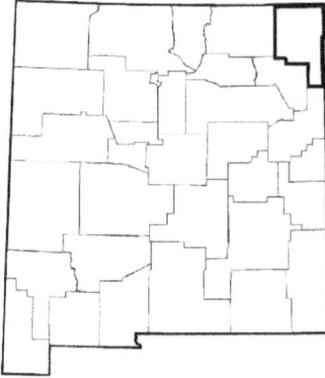

Union County was created in 1903. The Union County Courthouse was built in 1909 in Clayton, the county's seat.

County Seat: Clayton

Communities: Folsom, Des Moines, Stead, Grenville, Mt. Dora, Capulin, Gladstone and Amistad

3,831 Square Miles

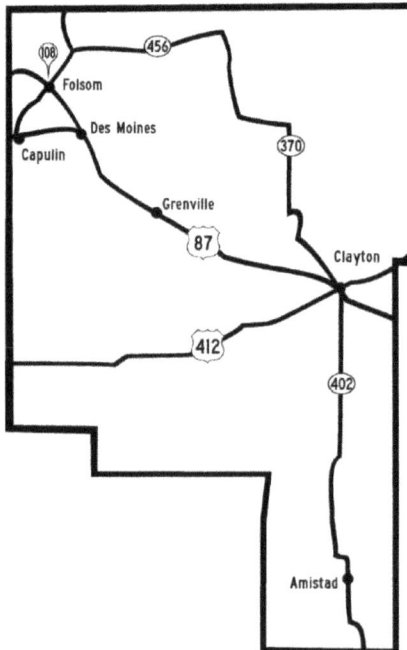

SARAH "SALLY" J. ROOKE
(1843 – 1908)

On the night of August 27, 1908, while working as a telephone operator, Sally received a call that a wall of water was rushing down the dry Cimarron River towards Folsom. She perished that stormy night at her switchboard warning of the danger, saving countless lives. Telephone operators across the country contributed 4,334 dimes to honor their colleague with a memorial.

In 1905, at the age of 65, Sally Rooke came to New Mexico from her home in Preston, Iowa, to visit her friend, Virginia Morgan. She loved the climate, the beauty of the land, and the skies of New Mexico, deciding to stay and become a homesteader. She also became the telephone operator in the Folsom office of the Des Moines Telephone Company.

On August 27, 1908, at around midnight, Mrs. Rooke received a warning call that heavy rain was impacting the dry Cimarron River's headwaters, turning it into a water wall heading toward the village of Folsom. Mrs. Rook stayed at her switchboard, calling the telephone service subscribers to warn them to get out of their homes. Ignoring her safety, she continued to call and plead with the people. She perished in the flood at the age of 68.

Installation Site
NM 325 at the Junction of NM 456 on the west side of Folsom Museum

· Valencia County ·

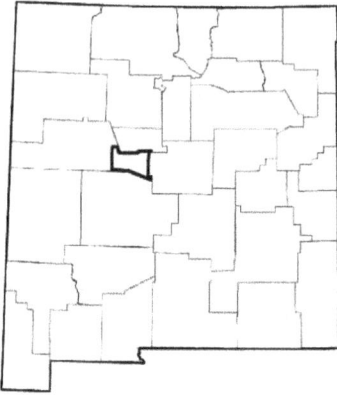

Valencia County was created in 1852 by Mexico, as one of the nine original counties for the territorial legislature. It is named for the Village of Valencia.

County Seat: Los Lunas

Communities: Belen, Los Chaves, Bosque Farms, Jarales, Valencia, Vegita and Tome

1,458 Square Miles

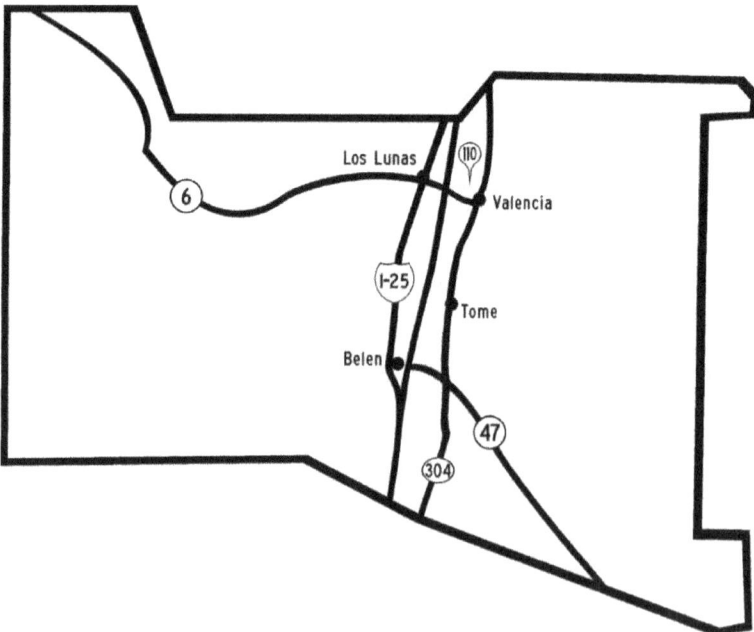

SITE OF LOS PINOS HACIENDA

During the 1830s, Los Pinos Hacienda on the Camino Real was the home of José Mariano Chávez and his wife, Dolores Perea. Chávez was acting governor of New Mexico for two and a half months in 1844. Upon his death, Dolores married the prosperous merchant Henry Connelly, the territorial governor of New Mexico during the Civil War. Confederate troops briefly occupied Los Pinos during the Battle of Peralta on April 15, 1862. By the mid-1920s, the house located near this marker had been destroyed.

Bosque de Los Pinos was created in 1769 when floods caused the Rio Grande to change. Los Pinos Hacienda is located eighteen miles south of Albuquerque near the village of Peralta. The military post was established there in May 1862 on land leased from Territorial Governor Henry Connelly. The camp was a supply depot and a staging area for Navajo campaigns. The soldiers at Los Pinos scouted for Indians, retrieved stolen stock, performed escort duty, and helped maintain public order.

Installation site
NM Highway 47 - near Los Piños Road
in Bosque Farms

Additional Resources

Bernalillo County Resources

History of Bernalillo County
The Sandoval County Historical Society Center for SW Research.

History of New Mexico by Charles Coan, 1993.

Centuries of Santa Fe by Paul Horgan, 1992.

New Mexico in Maps by University of New Mexico Professor Jerry L. Wilson. *Albuquerque* by Marc Simmons, 1988.

History of Alameda
Albuquerque's North Valley: Alameda & Los Ranchos by Francelle E Alexander, Rio Grande Books, December 2017.

History of Albuquerque
A City at the End of the World by Vincent Barrett Price, Albuquerque, University of New Mexico Press, 1992.

A History Lover's Guide to Albuquerque (History & Guide) by Roger M. Zimmerman, Charleston, South Carolina, History Press, October 2019.

Albuquerque: 100 Years in Pictures, 1875-1975 by George Fitzpatrick and Harvey Caplin, Albuquerque, Calvin Horn Publisher, 1975.

As I Remember Albuquerque by George Dolittle, Aiken Printing, 1973.

Historic Albuquerque Today: An Overview Survey of Historic Buildings and Districts, by Susan DeWitt, Historic Landmarks Survey of Albuquerque, 1978.

Making the Most of It: Public Works in Albuquerque During the Great Depression 1929-1942, by Charles Biebel, Albuquerque: The Albuquerque Museum, 1986.

Old Town Albuquerque, New Mexico: A Guide to its History and Architecture by Byron Johnson, Albuquerque, Albuquerque City, 1980.

The Stories Behind the Street Names of Albuquerque, Santa Fe and Taos by Don Gill, Chicago, Bonus Books, Inc., 1994.

History of Camp Albuquerque
Axis Invasion of the American West: POWs in New Mexico, 1942-1946, in the New Mexico Historical Review, April 1974.

History of Doña Elena Gallegos
Elena Gallegos
Albuquerque's North Valley, Volume 2, by Francelle E. Alexander The second volume chronicles the history of the village of Alameda and the villages of the Elena Gallegos Land Grant, including Los Ranchos, 2017.

History of Flamenco - Dance of Passion
The Spirit of Flamenco: From Spain to New Mexico by Nicolasa M. Chavez, Albuquerque, Museum of New Mexico Press, 2015.

History of Josefa Baca
Pajarito Land Grant
Pajarito Land Grant: A Contextual Analysis of Its Confirmation by the U.S. Government by Elaine Patricia Lujan, The Natural Resources Journal, 2008.

History of Crossroads at Martineztown
Martineztown- 1823-1950: Hispanics, Italians, Jesuits & Land Investors in New Town Albuquerque By Joseph P. Sanchez and Larry D. Miller, Albuquerque, Rio Grande Books, November 2009.

Catron County Resources

Agnes Morley Cleaveland
Open Range: The Life of Agnes Morley Cleaveland by Darlis A. Miller, University of Oklahoma Press, 2010.

Women of the West by Dorothy, Gray, Les Femmes Publisher, 1976.

No Life for a Lady by Agnes Morley Cleaveland, University of Nebraska Press, 1977.

Chaves County Resources

The Roswell Incident
The Roswell Incident by Charles Berlitz and William L. Moore, New York, Grosset & Dunlap, 1980.

The UFO Invasion - The Roswell Incident, Alien Abductions, and Government Coverups by Kendrick Frazier, Barry Karr and Joe Nickell, Prometheus, 1997.

The Women of Shakespeare
The Hill Family of Shakespeare; How a Cowboy and a Schoolmarm Got Married and Saved a Historic Ghost Town by Janaloo Hill, Self-Published, 2001.

Cibola County Resources

Susie Rayos Marmon
No additional resources located.

Colfax County Resources

First Automobile in New Mexico
No additional resources located.

Maxwell Land Grant

The Maxwell Land Grant, by Jim Berry Pearson, Norman, Oklahoma, University of Oklahoma Press, 1961.

Maxwell Land Grant: A New Mexico Item by William Aloysius Keleher, University of New Mexico Press, 1984.

Translating Property: The Maxwell Land Grant and the Conflict over Land in the American West, 1840-1900 by Maria E. Montoya, University of California Press, 2002.

Tessie Maxwell of the Maxwell Land Grant Family by Louis Serna, Self-Published, 2012.

Curry County Resources

Lincoln-Jackson School
No additional resources located.

Norman Petty Recording Studios
Curry County, New Mexico: Including its History, The Hotel Clovis, The Norman Petty Recording Studios, The Caprock Escarpment, and More by Johnathan Black, Earth Eyes Travel Guides, 2012.

The King of Clovis by Frank Blanas, United Kingdom, Rollercoaster Books, 2014.

DeBaca County Resources

Helene Haack Allen
Living Water: Our Mid-Pecos History - the Families & Events from Fort to Future by Bob Parsons, Mid-Pecos Historical Foundation, 1983.

Doña Ana County Resources

Jornada del Muerto
Geology of Jornada del Muerto Coal Field, Socorro County, New Mexico Circular 168, by D.E. Tabet, Socorro, New Mexico: New Mexico Bureau of Mines & Mineral,1979.

Maria Gutiérrez Spencer
The Community Can Be Sold on Spanish by Maria Gutiérrez de Prieto, New Mexico School Review, April 1, 1952.

Paraje San Diego
No additional resources located.

Site of San Agustin Springs
No additional resources located.

Eddy County Resources

Carlsbad Caverns National Park
Carlsbad Caverns National Park by John Barnett, Carlsbad Caverns Natural History Association. 1969.

Carlsbad Caverns National Park New Mexico Its Early Explorations by Jim White, Chicago, Genuine Curteich, 1951.

Carlsbad and Carlsbad Caverns (Images of America) by Charles B. Eddy, Arcadia Publishing, 2010.

Potash Discovery at McSweeney-McNutt
Economic Geology of the Carlsbad Potash District, New Mexico by George S. Austin and James M. Barker, Geo Science World, 1990.

Grant County Resources

Anita Scott Coleman
Unfinished Masterpiece: The Harlem Renaissance Fiction of Anita Scott Coleman by Anita Scott Coleman, Laurie Champion and Bruce A. Glasrud, Editors, Texas Tech University, 2008.

Western Echoes of the Harlem Renaissance: The Life and Writings of Anita Scott Coleman, Verner D. Mitchell and Cynthia Davis, Editors, University of Oklahoma Press, 2008.

Gila, New Mexico – Lyons & Campbell
Ranch Headquarters
Triumph and Tragedy – A History of Tom Lyons & the LCs by Ida Foster Campbell and Alice Foster Hill, High-Lonesome Books, 2003.

The Death of Mangas Coloradas
Apaches: A History and Culture Portrait, by James Haley, University of Oklahoma Press, 1997.

Mangas Coloradas: Chief of the Chiricahua Apaches by Edwin R. Sweeney, University of Oklahoma Press, 1998.

MIMBRES VALLEY
Between Mimbres and Hohokam: Exploring the Archaeology and History of Southeastern Arizona and Southwestern New Mexico by Henry D. Wallace, Desert Archaeology, 2014.

Guadalupe County Resources

Vásquez de Coronado's Route
Desert Drums: The Pueblo Indians of New Mexico, 1540-1928 by Leo Crane, Little, Brown, 1928.

North American Exploration by John Logan Allen, University of Nebraska Press, 1997.

The Coronado Expedition to Tierra Nueva: The 1540-1542 - Route across the Southwest by Richard Flint and Shirley Cushing Flint, University Press of Colorado, 2004.

Harding County Resources

Monica and Carlotta Gallegos
No additional resources located.

Hidalgo County Resources

No additional resources located.

Lea County Resources

Hobbs Army Airfield
Hobbs Army Airfield: Army Air Forces Flying Training Command by Charles D. Baylis, Army and Navy Publishing Co., 1943.

Hobbs Discovery Well
Discovery Wells by Charles R. Lewis, Austin, Texas, Privately Published, 1993.

The Story of the American Oil Industry: Brine to Bonanza, by Kathleen Crotty Abrams, Pioneer Publications Inc., 1981.

Lincoln County Resources

Susan McSween Barber
In the Shadow of Billy the Kid: Susan McSween and the Lincoln County War by Kathleen P. Chamberlain, University of New Mexico Press, 2013.

Violence in Lincoln County 1869-188 by William A. Kelleher, University of New Mexico Press, 1957.

Los Alamos County Resources

Marjorie Bell Chambers, Ph.D.
Marjorie Bell Chambers Memoir, by Marjorie Bell Chambers, Publisher Unknown, 1987.

Peggy Pond Church
Bones Incandescent: The Pajarito Journals of Peggy Pond Church by Shelley Armitage, Texas Tech University Press, 2001.

At Home on the Slopes of Mountains: The Story of Peggy Pond Church by Sharon Snyder, Los Alamos Historical Society Publication, 2001.

Luna County Resources

First Aero Squadron Airfield
Cradle of Airpower: An Illustrated History of Maxwell Air Force Base 1918–2018, by Air University Press, Jerome A. Ennels, et al., 2019.

Mary Ann Deming Crocker
The Place Names of New Mexico. Albuquerque, New Mexico, Robert Julyan, University of New Mexico Press, 1998.

New Mexico's Railroads: A Historical Survey. Albuquerque, New Mexico, by David F. Myrick, University of New Mexico Press, 1990.

McKinley County Resources

Olla Maidens – Zuni Pueblo
Pueblo Nations: Eight Centuries of Pueblo Indian History by Joe S. Sando, Santa Fe, New Mexico, Clear Light Publishers, 1998.

Mora County Resources

St. Vrain Mill – Ceran St. Vrain
Mansfield on the Condition of the Western Forts, 1853-54 by Robert W. Frazer, Norman, Oklahoma, 1963.

Otero County Resources

Three Rivers Petroglyph Site
Three Rivers Petroglyph Site: Results of the ASNM Rock Art Recording Field School by Meliha S. Duran and Helen K. Crotty. Archaeology Society of New Mexico, January 1, 1999.

Images from the Past: Rock Art: A Self-Guided Tour of Petroglyphs and Pictographs of the American Southwest, by Robin Scott Bicknell, Tucson, Arizona, Patrice Press, 2001.

John Prather – "Mule King"
Sunshine and shadows in New Mexico's past – The Statehood Period, by Richard Melzer, Los Ranchos, New Mexico, Rio Grande Books, 2012.

John Prather by John Donald Robb, Center for Southwest Research, University of New Mexico, 1973.

"Miss Mac" – Pioneer Woman
Scots in the North American West, 1790–1917, by Fernec Morton Szasz, University of Oklahoma Press, 2000.

Pioneer Mountain
No additional resources located.

Turquoise
Ghost Towns Alive: Trips to New Mexico's Past by Linda G. Harris and Pamela Porter, University of New Mexico Press, 2003.

Quay County Resources

Yetta Kohn

Yetta Kohn's Legacy by Sharon Fried, Article published in New Mexico Jewish Historical Society Newsletter in December 2008.

Rio Arriba County Resources

Córdova

High Road to Taos by Mike Butler, Cordova, New Mexico, Arcadia Publishing, 2016.

Doña Margarita Martín, The Queens Of Aragon: Their Lives And Time by E. L. Miron, Port Washington, New York, Associated Faculty, 1970.

Los Luceros Hacienda

Historic Ranches of Northeastern New Mexico, by Baldwin G. Burr, Arcadia Publishing, 2016.

Navajo Lake State Park

Places. History, Legend, Landscape by Laurance Linford University of Utah Press, Salt Lake City, 2000.

Roosevelt County Resources

Buffalo Soldier Hill

The Buffalo Soldiers in The Indian Wars by Fairfax Davis Downey and Harold James, New York, McGraw-Hill, 1969.

Rose Powers White

No additional resources located.

Sandoval County Resources

Dulcelina Salce Curtis

No additional resources located.

San Juan County Resources

Navajo Lake State Park – San Juan River Quality Water Area
No additional resources located.

San Miguel County Resources

Glorieta Pass Battlefield
A Compendium of the War of the Rebellion by Frederick H. Dyer, Des Moines, Iowa, The Dyer Publishing Company,1908.

The Battle of Glorieta Pass: A Gettysburg in The West, March 26-28, 1862, by Thomas S. Edrington and John Taylor, Albuquerque, New Mexico, University of New Mexico Press,1998.

Santa Fe County Resources

Galisteo Basin – Southern Rockies
The Galisteo Basin and Cerrillos Hills, by Paul R. Secord and Homer E. Milford, Arcadia Publishing, 2018.

Hispanic Women of Colonial New Mexico and Marriage
Doña Fracisca Gómez Robledo
Maldonado Journey to the Kingdom of New Mexico – Descendants of Juan López de Godoy by Gilbert Maldonado, Trafford Publishing, 2014.

Inez Bushner Gill
Legislative apportionment and congressional districting in New Mexico, by Inez Bushner Gill, Publications of the Division of Government Research, University of New Mexico, 1953.

Maralyn Budke
No additional resources located.

Route 66
Legendary Route 66: A Journey Through Time Along America's Mother Road by Michael Witzel, St. Paul, Minnesota, Voyageur Press Publishing, 2007.

Virginia Gutierrez
Talking with the Clay: The Art of Pueblo Pottery in the 21st Century, by Stephen Trimble, Native Arts and Voices, 2007.

Pueblo Pottery Families, by Lillian Peaster, Schiffer Books, 2003.

Hispanic Women of Colonial New Mexico and the Law
Doña Antonia Moraga
Spanish Colonial Women and the Law by Linda Tigges, Santa Fe, New Mexico, Sunstone Press, 2017.

Hispanic Women of Colonial New Mexico and the Law
Doña Rosa Bustamante
Spanish Colonial Women and the Law by Linda Tigges, Santa Fe, New Mexico, 2017. Sunstone Press, 2017.

Hispanic Women of Colonial New Mexico and Land Ownership
Vega y Coca Sisters – Feliciana, Leonardo, Maria, Francisca and Isabel
The Spanish Recolonization of New Mexico by Jose Antonio Esoqiubel, Hispanic Genealogical Research Center of New Mexico, 1999.

Sierra County Resources

Caballo Mountains
Geology of the Caballo Mountains by William R. Seager and Greg H. Mack, Ohio State University, 2003.

Elephant Butte Dam
Elephant Butte Dam by Sherry Fletcher and Cindy Carpenter, Charleston, South Carolina, Arcadia Publishing, 2015.

Jornada Del Muerto
Jornada Del Muerto: A Pageant of the Desert by Brodie Crouch by Arthur H. Clark, University of Oklahoma Press, 1989.

Magnolia Ellis
Reflections by William H. White, Published by Amazon, 2012.

Socorro County Resources

Carthage – Tokay – Fraley
Mining history of the Carthage Coal Field, Socorro County, New Mexico by Gretchen K. Hoffman and Joseph P. Hereford, Published by New Mexico Geological Society, 2009.

Kelly
No additional resources located.

New Mexico Tech
No additional resources located.

Socorro
Socorro: The Heart of New Mexico by Barbara R. DuBois, Albuquerque, New Mexico, Mercury HeartLink, 2015.

Territorial History of Socorro, New Mexico by Bruce Ashcroft by Texas Western Press, 1988.

Taos County Resources

Rio Costilla Valley
No additional resources located.

Torrance County Resources

Homesteader Mary Ellen "Mollie"

Hall Warren Klapp
No additional resources located.

Union County Resources

Sarah "Sally" J. Rooke
From Martyrs to Murderers: The Old Southwest's Saints, Sinners & Scalawags by Jacqueline Dorgan Meketa, Yucca Tree Press, 1993.

Valencia County Resources

Site of Los Pinos Hacienda
El Camino Real De Tierra Adentro National Historic Trail Comprehensive Management Plan, Author and Publisher Unknown, Appendix E, Page 208.

About the Authors

Phil T. Archuletta is a native New Mexican, born in the town of El Rito, located in Rio Arriba County.

He is one of the founders of Ojo Caliente Craftsman, one of the largest manufacturers in Northern New Mexico during the 1970s and 1980s. Today, he is the Chief Executive Officer of P & M Signs, Inc. located in Mountainair, New Mexico. His clients include the U. S. Forest Service, National Park Service, the Department of Game and Fish, Bureau of Land Management, the New Mexico Department of Transportation, and cities, counties and municipalities throughout the United States. He has the distinction of having one of the few Smokey Bear franchises in the country. You can find his signs throughout the entire U.S. Forest Service and National Park system.

He is the co-author of *By the Grace of God – Stories from the American Dream* and *Women Marked for History*, which won the New Mexico Heritage Preservation Award in 2015. He is also the author of *Traveling New Mexico* published in 2004.

In addition to his "day job," Phil has been inventing and patenting products throughout his lifetime. He has five patents including an anti-vandalism hardware device known as the "Tuffnut."

Rosanne Roberts Archuletta was born in Philadelphia and raised near the Pocono Mountains of Pennsylvania, in a small town called Bangor.

She spent most of her adult life living and creating a business in San Francisco. As a volunteer, she was on the Board and was an Instructor and Business Coach at the Renaissance Entrepreneurship Center for nearly a decade.

Since 1989, she has been the Principal of R.M. Roberts and Associates, a human resources consulting firm. Her firm provides training and coaching, staff recruiting and business consulting to organizations throughout the United States.

She is also a dynamic speaker who has lectured nationally on topics related to professional and personal development. She was a speaker at the United Nations' conference on the status of women held in Beijing, China in 1995. She was also a speaker at the Pennsylvania State University's College of Liberal Arts' Career Day.

She is the co-author of *By the Grace of God – Stories from the American Dream* and *Women Marked for History,* which won the New Mexico Heritage Preservation Award in 2015. Rosanne holds a M.A. degree from Naropa University and a B.A. degree from The Pennsylvania State University. Her Master's thesis, "Mystics in the Boardroom: Creating a Life Enriching Workplace," reflects her passion for her work.

Learn more now at:

www.travelingnewmexico.com
www.pmsignsinc.com
www.womenmarkedforhistory.com

www.ingramcontent.com/pod-product-compliance
Lightning Source LLC
Chambersburg PA
CBHW070042100426
42740CB00013B/2764